What you hold in your hand is a precious jewel. The message of His presence, of His love, and living a life of laid down love permeate the pages of this work. Written from Lana's own journey and diary of heavenly oracles, this work is a manual for a company of people in this hour who desire to deny themselves, take up their cross and journey deeper into the heart of Heaven. I can only say wonderful things about this book and it's author!

—Daniel Black, Lover
of Jesus
Grace Like A River Ministries

Lana Vawser in *Desperately Deep* echoes the longing of many Christians that I meet, a deep desire for more intimacy with their Saviour Jesus Christ. But the book is more than that; it is a practical, timely book and full of gems to be dipped into often. Psalm 20:4

—Pastor Don Hobbs,
Senior Pastor Shire
West Christian Church Menai,
Sydney, Australia

When a person decides to get serious with God that person can expect God to respond. Desperately Deep is the result of a young woman's plunge into the deep end. This may be a short read, but not a shallow read. It is unique in style and reads not unlike devotional. The truths that come through the pages are both personal to the writer and yet challenging for any of us. Any person who desires to go deep into God will find more than enough meat in Lana's book to keep them feasting for a long time!

—Jerry Praetzel
International Bible Teacher

Desperately Deep

Desperately Deep

Developing Deep
Devotion and Dialogue
with Jesus

Lana Vawser

First Published, 2009, by Tate Publishing & Enterprises, LLC
127 E. Trade Center Terrace | Mustang, Oklahoma 73064 USA 1.888.361.9473 |
www.tatepublishing.com

Republished, 2017, by Lana Vawser Ministries
PO Box 241, Coolum Beach, Qld 4573,

Religion: Christian Life: Personal Growth

Dedication

To my best friend, my reason for living, my Lord and Savior, Jesus Christ. It is all for you, for the glory of your name.

To my husband, Kevin, my soul mate, my confidant, and my ministry partner—I love you. Thank you for supporting me, drawing and leading me closer to Jesus every day. You are the man of my dreams.

Table of Contents

Contents

Introduction

It is amazing when you venture into a new chapter of your life that you never thought you would enter. This book is my new chapter. I never imagined myself writing a book. However, as I sit before my computer, I am excited. I believe that Jesus has given me some amazing jewels and priceless treasures straight from his heart for you. They are to bless you, encourage you, equip you, and propel you deeper into relationship with Him and release you to equip others.

This very topic is on the heart of God. He desires each of his children to come deeper into intimate relationship with Him and learn to hear his voice above all else. In the Western church, it seems that we have not relied upon the Spirit as much as we should. Many seem to have turned away from desperation for deeper intimacy with Him, to hear his voice ourselves. Instead, we have trusted others to receive the manna from heaven for us on our behalf.

God desires for us to learn to walk in relationship with Him knowing his great love for us and how to hear his voice for ourselves. He wants this above all else, and he is willing to speak to us on an ongoing basis. Jesus does not speak to a select few but to *all* who seek Him. He speaks to each of us in many ways. It is up to us to learn to fine tune our ears to hear what he is saying to us. Then we must take what he says and move forward.

In the body of Christ, as we learn to hear his voice and know his love, we will grow in greater levels of intimacy, revelation, discernment, and authority. Who wouldn't want to learn how to hear the voice of the Almighty God?

You will notice two main threads in this book: the call flowing from the heart of Jesus for deeper intimacy with Him, going deeper in knowing his love for you and the art of hearing his voice.

The purpose of this book is to encourage each one of us to plunge continually deeper into all that God has for us, to truly walk the abundant life he purchased for us, whilst recognising it is not a guide full of religious dos and *don'ts* or a manual to show us how much we fall short and propel us into condemnation. It is an encouragement to continue growing in relationship with Him and to learn areas we can continue to grow in that take us deeper into a holy life. We are already holy, accepted, loved, cherished, and valued, and as the body of Christ, we must continue to walk in the fullness of our true identity.

This book reflects a journey that I have walked over quite a few years and was not a journey that happened miraculously overnight. So do not be discouraged or disheartened if the journey takes longer than you expect. My journey will not be your journey. It may have similarities, but it will not be exactly the same. This book contains jewels I believe God has given me, and it is my heart to share them with you to see you grow closer to Jesus, deeper in his love, further in faith, and more and more full of his joy as you seek Him. If you think about it, this journey we are on, of growing closer to Jesus and growing in faith, is for all of our earthly lives.

Let's embark on this journey together. The Spirit is here, he is longing to speak, and his arms are wide open to embrace you and take you to a level you have never experienced before.

Are you willing to walk into his arms, forever leave behind the old, and walk into the new? To feel his love more intimately, know his voice more deeply, and strengthen your relationship with Him? I share with you what I have experienced thus far. There is nothing sweeter than deeper fellowship with the Lord of the heavens and the earth—Jesus Christ. I am sure you will agree.

Let's go!

—Lana Vawser

Surrendered Heart

I don't know about you, but I used to cringe when I heard the word *surrender*. I thought that it was a painful experience where you lay down all the things *you* wanted so that God could give you what he wanted. In my early days of experiencing intimacy with Jesus, I thought that he was not going to give me what I wanted. I also thought what he gave me would not be as good as what I had asked for or planned. Wrong view of God! We must all examine what we believe about God in the light of what his Word says; we must repent of any belief that is contrary to his Word and ask for his truth. That has been the story of my life thus far. Seriously, looking back on that now, I just laugh and thank God for his grace. He is so good and loving and that which he gives us is so much better than anything we could ever imagine.

Jesus said something to me a few years ago, and it changed my life and the way that I thought. He said to me, "Lana, if you live your life with a closed hand, you cannot release anything to me, nor can I give you anything in return. Your grip on everything does not allow my Spirit the room to move. Do you know what your closed hand says to me, Lana? It says that you do not trust me. Daughter, listen to me, I love you and will give you what is best for you and will bless you in ways you have never dreamed. All you need to do is open your hand and keep it open."

Those words transformed my thinking and convicted my heart to the core. Not only was it a surrender issue that God was calling me to, but it was an issue of trust. If I truly trusted who Jesus was, how could I ever not believe he would provide for me? If I believe Jesus is all loving and good, then would he not give me what is best? Complete surrender means having a revelation of the goodness, faithfulness, and love of Jesus and knowing he will give us what is *best*.

I received a word spoken to me by the Spirit for the bride of Christ on June 24, 2007. It speaks of the very heart of God for our surrender.

Beautiful Surrender

I am calling many of you to a time of great surrender. I am calling many of you individually and corporately to lay down things that you would have never expected to give up. I am calling many of you to walk forth with open hands. Allow me to take from your life that which I desire, and I will replace it with something much more beautiful.

I ask many of you to cultivate a heart of surrender. Cultivate this attitude in your life. Do not let surrender be a season or a moment in your life, but a daily action.

Do not worry about what I am asking you to lay down, for when I ask you to release something, I am giving you the grace to release it. It will indeed bring you to a deeper place of fellowship, brokenness, and intimacy with me.

I am doing a major work in many upcoming leaders at this time. It will be a time of great refining, a time of fire, and a time of trial. It will be a time that I will teach many about wisdom in ways they would never have understood previously.

When I ask each of you to release something to me, release it with a surrendered heart. Release it without giving into flesh speaking out how hard it is. Do not speak how much the flesh is rising up or how much pain it is causing you to release this. Instead, step forth and release. Step forth and gladly lay down all at my throne. Know that I am developing great trust and character within each of you.

Now is the time for promotion within my church. I am raising many up in the midst of surrender. In the midst of surrender, many of you who think that you are losing are actually gaining. If I call you to step back, you will then step forward in another area you did not realize.

The heavens have opened, and the

supernatural power from my heart is pouring upon those who have their hands open. It is pouring on those whose hearts are willing to receive and those whose hearts are ready for the harvest. You may feel you are going into a time of decline, but I declare and decree that you are going into a time of incline! Let not your reward be earthly, but let your reward be heavenly, for there the true reward is.

Jesus calls us to walk a life of surrender. Not as a hard task master asking us to surrender or be punished, but to surrender to his loving ways and nature and be released into a greater abundant life.

"Then Jesus said to his disciples 'If anyone would come after me, let him deny himself and take up his cross and follow me.'" Matthew 16:24 (cev)

What does Matthew 16:24 mean to you? This verse implies that one is to deny himself. We are to lay ourselves down and love and care for others as Jesus did. However, the main concept here is to *deny* oneself. The word used here could have also been surrender. If we want to follow Jesus, we must surrender our life, mind, will, body, heart, emotions, and plans to Jesus. It is in that place of total surrender to Jesus that we will find depth of intimacy.

Yet what is the key? You really need to know and believe the goodness and faithfulness of Jesus Christ. What is your view of Jesus? Do you view Jesus through the lens of past hurts or past experiences? Or do you truly see Him for all that the Word says that he is? Loving, faithful, compassionate, etc.

It is imperative that as Christians we have a correct view of Jesus. In my own experience, I viewed Jesus as an authoritarian who would be extremely angry if you stepped one foot out of line. That was a wrong view of Him, and it was a result of my life experience with male figures. That wrong concept caused me many years of torment and unsettling because no matter what I ever did for Jesus, I felt I could never do anything good enough. I missed the whole concept of grace and God's extraordinary love for me, and how amazingly special I was to Him! I viewed Jesus through extremely distorted lenses. My freedom came through a lot of time in his presence, repenting for these wrong beliefs, inviting his revelation of his amazing love into my heart, and not giving up until I started to see a change. It is still   a journey day by day to know the Lord's amazing love, but now I am partnered with Him and not walking away from Him. Partnering with Jesus means agreeing with what the Word says about Him, and deciding what you believe, to then change what you think (Philippians 4:8), and let Him show you his heart for you.

I did not understand the concept of "being" and "not doing." I did not know that Jesus loved me unconditionally and accepted me because of who I was instead of for what I did for Him. Many within the Western church today find themselves in the same boat. Many are not walking in the freedom of knowing who they really are, but are caught up in works of religion to gain acceptance from Jesus.

A surrendered heart is a heart that is not striving, that is settled in God's love. It is a heart that knows his love, its value in Jesus, and its acceptance. Believe me; I know that this is a battle that can feel bigger than a mountain. I've walked it and am still walking it out. The more I walk through this journey of knowing his love, my identity and value, the more I see how imperative it is in our walk with Jesus. If any of these foundational blocks are out of line, it affects the entire relationship.

Think about it. If you do not know his love and who you are in Christ, then you will not walk in peace, life abundant, and the power to which he has called you. You will not walk in the abundant intimacy with Him, life he has called you to, and authority that is already yours. You will not walk in the freedom purchased for you at Calvary. It will be but a mere drop in your life instead of a flooding ocean.

"Praise the God and Father of our Lord Jesus Christ for the spiritual blessings that Christ has brought us from heaven!" Ephesians 1:3 (cev)

"Blessed be the God and Father of our Lord Jesus Christ, who has blessed us in Christ with every spiritual blessing in the heavenly places." Ephesians 1:3 (esv)

"This was according to the eternal purpose that he has realized in Christ Jesus our Lord, in whom we have boldness and access with confidence through our faith in Him." Ephesians 3:11–12 (esv)

Jesus' desire is for us to walk in our inheritance—all that we have been given through the precious death and resurrection of Jesus Christ. What a marvelous act of love he accomplished for us at Calvary. It has set us free for all the days of our lives, and it gives us every spiritual blessing in the heavenlies. However, it does that only as we access it and walk in it.

There are too many defeated Christians around. Too many Christians are walking around with their heads down allowing the enemy to walk all over them. They allow life to throw circumstances at them that crumble them, instead of standing firm. Then their responses keep them from walking in the fullness of all Christ purchased at Calvary. Peace, joy, freedom, victory, forgiveness, and freedom from condemnation are all possible for each of us. Nevertheless it is our choice to walk in these things because it was already *all* given to us through Christ.

When we do not believe who Jesus says we are and we are caught in the trap of doing things to please God, we are living outside fullness we were given at the cross. When we do not align ourselves with the truth of who God says we are and our identity in Christ, inviting the Holy Spirit to come and reveal the truth to us, we place ourselves in bondage to the enemy and all his lies about God and us. As believers I believe we are to continue to invite the Holy Spirit to come and uproot the weeds of lies that have taken root in our hearts about who He says we are and who He is. If we do not "catch the troubling foxes" that come to raid our vineyard of intimacy (Songs of Songs 2) and allow the lies of the enemy to take root, we end up exhausted, discouraged, and in bondage. We will end up crawling exhausted over the finish line to enter heaven because we have spent our lives trying to work our way there by our works instead of *leaping victoriously* into the promised land. That is not God's heart for us. We are called to live in the abundant life that Jesus spoke of in John 10:10. To live in the completed work of the Cross. Our identity and our authority. Living daily in the revelation that God is good, He is kind, He is loving and He delights in you and I. I want to encourage you today to make a choice to continue to ask the Holy Spirit to reveal His truth to you and lead you deeper into the revelation of your identity and the JOY that is found in the awakening of being children of God. May we be people that one day enter into Glory, eternity with Him from a life lived in fullness and walking in a depth of revelation of his love, instead of crawling over the line beaten and bruised and discouraged.

Jesus said something to me once: "Lana, everyone surrenders to something whether they know me or not. Surrender is built within every human being because I placed it there." That really started me thinking. Everybody does surrender to something. We may surrender to Jesus or to our desire for success. We may surrender to our fleshly desires or our unhealthy thought patterns. We may surrender to our past abuse, pain, or heartache we have carried for a long time or we surrender to the circumstances we walk. No matter where we find ourselves in our lives, we will see that each one of us surrenders to something. It is that something that we need to identify. To what do you surrender your heart?

Every moment of every day each of us have a choice as to what we will surrender to. Every day we are faced with opportunities from Jesus, the enemy, and our flesh, which call us to surrender to them. We must always try to maintain our defense against the enemy. We must be people that are not ignorant of the devil's schemes (2 Corinthians 2:11) and when we have done all to stand, we continue to stand. Awake, present, engaged with the Word of God and taking our thoughts captive, and tearing down anything that raises itself up against the knowledge of who He is (2 Corinthians 10:4-5). We must live our lives capturing our thoughts, rather than allowing them to capture us. When we have insecure views of who we are, bad thought patterns, wrong heart motives, fleshly desires or sins, we may inadvertently surrender ourselves to our flesh or to the enemy, whether we like it or not.

The Spirit said to me, "Lana, in the life of every human being, there are decisions being brought before them all the time. The decisions made then determine whether they are aligning themselves under me or the enemy. There is no middle ground. That to which people surrender themselves, and that with which people align themselves, will open the doors for that spiritual atmosphere to flood their lives. It is all about surrender and alignment."

When these words were spoken to me, I had a picture in my mind of doors above our lives. Every time we surrender to something of God, the door opens and He pours out on us. However, if we surrender to that which is not of God, we open the door to the wrong spiritual atmosphere that comes along with it.

Now that does not mean that every time we make a

wrong choice or surrender our hearts to something not of God, that we are forever flooded with the wrong spiritual atmosphere. There is a reversal. If we surrender our hearts to the enemy in some way and that wrong door is opened, repentance slams that door shut again. The blood of Jesus covers us when we confess and repent, and his forgiveness closes that door.

We must be mindful of surrendering our hearts and continue to place our lives under the lordship of Jesus Christ and his Word. We must walk with Jesus every day, basking in his love. We must base our decisions upon the Word and continue to pray for the Spirit to enlighten us about how to live surrendered lives. Let us separate ourselves from things that do not glorify Jesus, and surrender ourselves only to that which He calls us. Let us continue to grow in the revelation that we are dearly loved, cherished, valued, forgiven, empowered, and accepted by Jesus himself, and then we will not easily surrender our hearts to things not of God.

Surrendering our hearts to Jesus daily is to have the heart attitude and prayer of:

"… not my will but yours be done." Luke 22:42b (esv)

To what are you surrendering your heart? Are you surrendering to what the Bible says you are? Or are you surrendering your heart to what the past has told you? Do you believe what people have told you about who you are? Or who God says you are? Do you surrender to what circumstances tell you?

Surrender in the area of identity and worth, circumstances or decision making is an everyday choice. Jesus is continually looking for those who will cry out, "Lord, not my will but yours be done," and take up their cross and follow him, no matter the cost.

Those who are close to the Lord and know his love will find themselves surrendering to him more and more, not necessarily because the Word says to but because it is a delight to surrender to someone you know loves you, cherishes you, and values you more than you could ever imagine. If you have trouble surrendering to the Lord, try spending more time in his presence, or talk to your pastor or trusted friend who can pray with you, but do not stop seeking out Jesus, even in little ways. Spend more time seeking out his Word. Ask the Spirit to change your heart, and He will. He wants to take us from glory to glory. In the New Testament glory means always having a good opinion concerning a person, resulting in praise, honor, and glory. It is something we receive when we learn the Word of God and walk in it. Glory also means the majesty of God.

Today and every day you are faced with a choice. To what will you surrender your heart? Which kingdom are you accessing? Are you accessing the kingdom that will never end and endures forever? Or are you accessing the kingdom of darkness that does not desire for you to grow? That kingdom desires to *"steal, kill, and destroy you"* (John 10:10, esv).

Let us be like Jesus who was so surrendered that He said, *"Father, not my will but yours be done... I only do what I see the Father doing"* (Luke 22:42b, John 5:19, esv).

If we walk in radical, deep intimacy with Jesus Christ holding surrender close to our hearts, then we will see the world changed. It will be changed only by those who truly walk in complete surrender to Jesus Christ.

Remember these things:

1. Be Positioned! Walk with Him in the cool of the day. You're your Garden with Jesus, your secret place, and linger with Him. The Lord is looking for those who will linger. Sit with Him. Enjoy Him, just be with Him, and invite the Holy Spirit to come and bring rest to your heart and soul by His kindness and love. Ask for more. As Heidi Baker says, "There is always more."

2. Continually pray for a deeper revelation of his love. Ask Him for a baptism of fire, the fire of His love to consume you.

3. Continue to live a life of leaning in and surrender. Ask the Holy Spirit to continue to teach you to live life with an open hand. Surrendered not only to His will, but His way, His process and KNOW that as you live your life with a heart that cries out "Teach Me your ways", "I yield", "I surrender", you will find yourself living a life in the BEST of all that He has for you. Don't fear the place of surrender, it's a place of JOY! For what He will give to you will be far greater than you have ever dreamed (Ephesians 3:20). Living life with a closed hand because of fear, limits us, robs our joy and keeps us from the land of ABUNDANCE that God has for us and all the blessings and breakthrough that await us.

4. Surrender and obedience go hand in hand. I want to encourage you to "keep short accounts" with the Lord. One thing I always attempt to do in my life is to live INTENTIONALLY and part of that intentionality is

"keeping short accounts with the Lord". I keep repentance close to my heart, and I am always inviting the Holy Spirit to teach me to remain sensitive to His leading and be QUICK to obey.

5. Ask him for a deeper revelation of who we are in Him and to reveal any lies and mindsets that don't align with the Word of God and who He says you are. Ask Him for His rhema truth to replace the lie, the trauma, the memory, the root of where the lies have taken hold. Invite the Holy Spirit to come and the fire of God to burn away the root of that lie by the revelation of His love.

6. All the things we need flow out of intimacy with Jesus Christ.

7. The more we see of Him, His goodness, His kindness and His love, the more we live a life of surrender and obedience, and it is not birthed out of a "slave mentality" that is attempting to "please God' or "keep Him happy", but it is the fruit of a life lived knowing the pleasure and delight of God and it is a JOY to surrender and obey.

I'm ready to go deeper, are you?

Prayer:
Father, thank you for your love. Thank you that you value me and love me more than anyone ever has or ever will. Lord, I ask that you would teach me to walk in surrender. Teach me how to grow in obedience to you.

Change my heart daily, Lord, so that I may always cry out, "Not my will, but yours be done."

Father, please forgive me for any way I have surrendered to the enemy through my thought patterns, sins, choices, self-doubt, or complacency. Teach me to align myself with you, your Word, and your kingdom.

Empower me to sacrifice and surrender anything you ask of me. Help me, Jesus, to remember intimacy with you is the key.

Show me who I am, Jesus. Show me how you think of me that I may be forever renewed in that revelation. In Jesus' name, amen.

Feasting

The topic of feasting is really interesting. We all are feasting on something in our lives. Whether we know Jesus as Lord or not, we are feasting every single day we are on this planet.

The American Heritage® Dictionary (2009) defines feasting as:

1.   Something giving great pleasure or satisfaction.

2.   To partake of a feast; eat heartily.

3.   To experience something with gratification or delight.

Do you know that what we feast on will affect our intimacy with Jesus? Within the church today we can often find ourselves feasting on things that do not bring life and sow life into our relationship with Jesus and others. He calls us to one world of serving, listening, and knowing him passionately. He does not want us to live a compromised life. He desires that we serve Jesus Christ alone.

It is very easy for us as Christians to fall into the trap of serving two masters. Having two masters means that we are living with one-foot following Jesus and the other fulfilling our fleshly, worldly desires. When we do this, we do not serve Jesus wholeheartedly. Walking with two masters makes following him very difficult. Try walking in a straight line while having each of your feet going in different directions. Walking becomes very difficult that way. In the natural, you will just go from side to side without walking forward. You will do the same thing in the spiritual. Today in the church, you will see many going from side to side.

A vision that I had encapsulates what I am trying to convey:

I found myself standing in a crowd of millions upon millions of people. All of us had shirts on that say "Jesus" across the front. As I looked around, I could see millions of fruit trees in the midst of all the people. These trees were all shapes and sizes. Suddenly Jesus appeared before the crowd and said, "Come; follow me."

A few others and I stepped forward. We who stepped forward followed him. As we walked toward huge white pearly gates, I heard the Spirit saying, "So few will come, so few will come." Such grief and sadness filled his voice.

I turned around and saw the millions we left behind who were all eating from the fruit trees. I then noticed each of the fruits had different words on them. They said, "materialism, money, self-fulfillment, pride, lust, or need for validation." Jesus stopped, looked at them, and said once more to them, "Come; follow me," but they turned their backs and focused on what they were eating from the trees.

My heart was so grieved that I could hardly breathe, but I continued to follow Jesus through the gates. He led us into a beautiful garden full of handsome fruit trees. These trees were unlike those outside. They glowed with a light the likes of which I had never before seen.

Jesus approached the trees and picked the fruit off them. He put it on a platter and brought it to us. We all ate and enjoyed. He then led us to a great banquet table where He said to us, "This is what I have prepared for you. Eat and be merry. Taste and see that I am good." That fellowship with Jesus Christ was indescribable.

Finally, He took each of us one by one and gave us charge over a flock of sheep. He told us that because we had been faithful, He had taken us farther into his kingdom. He said that because we had counted the cost, He was giving us the increase.

The last thing I saw was Jesus' face as He repeated, "So very few will come. So very few will come."

Romans 12:2 says that we are not to be conformed

to this world but transformed by the renewing of our minds (esv). We yield to his cleansing by the Word and receive renewed minds. We surrender to Jesus and spend time getting to know him. The result is that the worldly, fleshly desires and wounds fall away in the light of his glorious presence and love.

Those people in the vision did not hear Jesus calling them. They had not transformed their minds with the Word of God. If they had allowed the power of the Spirit to transform them, do you think they would have eaten evil fruit of the world?

We cannot be growing in deeper relationship with Jesus, flowing in the Spirit, walking in deep revelation of his love, and be close to his heart and still entertain things of this world. It is not possible. One glance at the heart of Jesus, and we are forever transformed. The things of the world grow dim and lifeless compared to the life and joy found in him. We are on a journey, which will be a continual process all the days of our lives, battling with our flesh like Paul did in Romans 7, but we must continue to delight in his presence daily and not be entertained by worldly lusts.

Keep in mind that Jesus does not look with condemnation upon those living in two worlds. He looks upon these with great love, yet a sense of sadness and compassion, a heart beating with the cry of wanting to lead them to a greater life that He purchased for them. Fortunately, He continues to call them closer to him. He wants them to let go of the things that hinder them. He works to build their relationship with him. He is constantly loving on them so they will repent and know him in a deeper way.

In the past when I have talked to Jesus about intimacy and relationship, He likens it as a dance. I follow his lead and look into his eyes. He draws me into a deep intimacy that is focused solely on him. I follow the Spirit, yet if I begin to look around or focus on something besides him, I trip and get out of step. Try dancing with someone and not surrendering to their lead, looking around and not focusing on them, you will end up fumbling all over the place.

Jesus wants us to feast on him as we look into his face through the Word, worship, and surrender. We will feast on his presence by spending time with him daily and be drawn closer than ever before and move from glory to glory. However, when we look around, we can be lured into a dance with other distractions such as the world and its beliefs and desires or our own fleshly wants.

We can so easily just put on our Jesus shirts to dance with the world, temptations the enemy offers us, and fleshly desires. We are called to be set apart and holy (1 Peter 1:16, esv). However, if we dance with the other things besides Christ, we are not being set apart and holy. Our Jesus shirts do not make us holy!

Here are a few ways to align ourselves with Jesus and follow his lead:

Mind

"And do not be conformed to this world, but be transformed by the renewal of your mind that by testing you may discern what is the will of God, what is good and acceptable and perfect." Romans 12:2 (esv)

Our minds are to be renewed by the Word of God (Ephesians 5), and we are to walk in the reality that we already have the mind of Christ (1 Corinthians 2:16). It is already ours because of what Jesus did on the cross by his death and resurrection. We simply need to walk in it (Ephesians 4:24, Colossians 3:10).

We must be careful with what we fill our minds. Our minds are like filing cabinets. We store everything in different files. As I have mentioned in previous chapters as we continue to filter what goes in and throw out things that are don't line up with what He says and His Word decrees over our lives, then we will find a greater level of living in victory in our minds and thinking on things that are lovely, kind and pure (Phillipans 4:8). The mind is a battlefield, but you have the victory in Christ. You have the mind of Christ (1 Corinthians 2:16) and I decree that as you take your thoughts captive and renew your mind, you will find a new level of freedom, divine insight and peace over your mind in Jesus name.

We do so much feasting in our minds that our thought patterns can lift us up or tear us down. Our thought patterns greatly affect our lives. They have the power to draw us closer to Jesus or lead us further away from him.

The secular world even teaches on the power of the mind to overcome. They call it the power of positive thinking. The world did not invent this. It started in the mind and heart of God when He created the power of thinking. God released that power into us when He created Adam and breathed life into him.

Think of the headlines and the magazines that we see on newsstands today. We see photos of stars stumbling out of nightclubs and reports of them cheating on their partners. When we read that information, it has the potential to influences our thoughts and spirit with things that are not pure. It definitely does not uplift our spirits. It does not help us keep the mind of Christ or draw us closer to Jesus. However, we so easily fill our minds with these things and somehow think they do not do us harm. Television and music have the same effect as the magazines. So why do we do it?

"Finally, brethren, whatever is true, whatever is honorable, whatever is right, whatever is pure, whatever is lovely, whatever is of good repute, if there is any excellence and if anything worthy of praise, dwell on these things." Philippians 4:8 (nasb)

If we look at this verse, we are given a checklist of what is to enter our minds to draw us closer to Jesus. These things are the things upon which we are to feast.

1. Whatever is true. (Factual, faithful, committed)

2. Whatever is honorable. (Morally upright)

3. Whatever is right. (Correct, proper)

4. Whatever is pure. (Virtuous)

5. Whatever is lovely. (Pleasing, caring, inspiring love)

6. Whatever is of good repute. (Good reputation)

7. Whatever is of excellence. (Superior quality)

8. Whatever is worthy of praise. (Worth admiration)

They are eight pointers to help us examine our thought lives, to filter our minds through these eight steps. If we are feasting upon things that do not match these eight pointers, we need to make a change.

Our minds are war zones. We must constantly be on our guard, fighting the good fight of faith. The good news is we have already overcome. We already have the victory over everything through Jesus Christ. We are to exercise that victory by walking in it; taking our thoughts captive. Our thoughts are going to come from one of three places:

1. God

2. The enemy

3. Our flesh

If a thought comes into my mind that I know is from my soul (the mind, will, and emotions), I consciously remove it by taking that thought captive and telling it to go. I will not surrender to it. I am not talking about daydreaming thoughts. We all have daydreams about harmless thoughts. I am talking about thoughts that hinder and draw us away from God.

If a thought comes into our minds that we recognize is harmful and not uplifting, we tell it to leave in Jesus' name. When the enemy plagues our minds with lies, doubts, and fears, we need to speak the Word of God aloud just as Jesus did when the enemy tempted him. I cannot tell you the number of times that a random thought will enter my mind, a thought not of my own, that would send fear raging through every part of my body. I once heard a voice tell me that I was going to get a brain tumor from God, and then after being in pain for a while, God would heal me for his glory. Can you imagine what that thought   did to me? It sent me into a spiral of fear and tormented thinking that the Lord would inflict such horrific pain upon me, simply to show his glory. At the moment of that fear, I had to stand against it with all the tools I was given in the Word. I quoted scripture and continued to surrender to God, knowing that He was good and that no matter what life would bring, He would not inflict harm upon his children just to show his glory. The Lord will use circumstances that we walk to bring forth his radiant love and glory, but this thought was not from God, so I stood firm and overcame.

When the enemy comes at me with the accusation, "Lana, God is so displeased with you, He does not accept you ..." I quote the Word right back at him. The Word of God says that I am accepted by the blood of the lamb, eternally loved, and I can approach the throne with boldness because of what Jesus Christ did for me at Calvary. Demons cannot stand the Word of God, so throw it at them at every opportunity given to you. Speak the Word to your flesh, use the Word at all times.

Lana Vawser

Jesus did it; we see Jesus overcoming the enemy three times in Scripture using the Word of God.

1. Forty days of fasting passed and Jesus was starving. Satan came to him and made an appealing suggestion: "If you are the Son of God, command this stone to become bread" (Luke 4:2–3 esv). Jesus responds, "Man shall not live by bread alone, but by every word that proceeds out of the mouth of God" (Luke 4:4, Deuteronomy 8:3 n k j v).

2. "And the devil took him up and showed him all the kingdoms of the world in a moment of time, and said to him, 'To you I will give all this authority and their glory, for it has been delivered to me, and I give it to whom I will. If you, then, will worship me, it will all be yours'" (Luke 4:5–7 esv). Jesus responds: "It is written; you shall worship the Lord your God and serve him only" (Luke 4:8 nasb).

3. And He led him to Jerusalem and had him stand on the pinnacle of the temple and said to him, "If you are the Son of God, throw yourself down from here. For it is written 'He will give his angels charge concerning you to guard you and on their hands, they will bear you up, lest you strike your foot against a stone.'" Luke 4:9–11 (nasb). Jesus responds, "It is said, you shall not put the Lord your God to the test" Luke 4:12 (nasb).

You and I are to walk and follow in the footsteps of Jesus, and He gives us the very model of how to go on a diet in our minds and feast only upon the Word of God. If we feast in our minds upon thoughts from our flesh or the enemy, we are simply contaminating ourselves.

Jesus showed me a vision about this whole thought process. I saw the thought come to the mind like a ticket. It would either be accepted or rejected. When the ticket was accepted, it went through the filter in the mind and the filing cabinet stored it. It then traveled down a chute, and then guess where it went ... to the heart!

Once a thought is in our mind and heart, it does not mean that it is there to stay. We can get it out. That is the amazing power of Jesus to cleanse and forgive. The point I am illustrating here is that your mind and heart are connected. Therefore, in a sense, what we allow in our minds feeds our hearts.

If our minds are full of things that are not in line with Philippians 4:8 and we need a massive clean out, here are some suggestions:

Ask the Holy Spirit to show you thought patterns and beliefs in your heart and mind that are not from him. Write them down. Write any lies you believe about yourself, condemnation from the past, tormenting thoughts, etc.

1.   Repent for believing each thought and lie. Ask the Holy Spirit to wash your heart and mind clean.

2.   Ask Jesus to replace those lies and thoughts with his Word. Ask Jesus for scripture concerning those lies and thoughts to replace them. Memorize those scriptures to get them into your heart and mind.

Jesus is the great gardener. Ask him to clean your heart and mind, and He will. He gladly will plant the most beautiful seeds of his Word in your heart and mind if you search his Word. Those seeds will sprout into beautiful flowers, fruitful thought processes, and beliefs. You will find yourself walking in a deeper revelation of Philippians 4:8 in your everyday life.

Yes, we will always battle with our minds while here on earth. However, with the empowerment of the Spirit, we will grow. We will surrender ourselves to feasting on what is good, pure, and lovely. As we grow in this area and go from glory to glory, we will become more like Jesus and walk with the mind of Christ. After all, we *already* have the mind of Christ; we just need to walk in it. Amen?

God wants you *full*.

God wants you *full*; He wants you full of his Word at all times. I decided to tag this encouragement on the end of this chapter, because even though I have touched on it at times during this chapter, I wanted to encourage you in your appetite for the Word of God.

Never ever stop feasting on God's Word. We are to feast on his Word every single day. It is our daily bread. We are to live daily by every word that flows from the heart of the Father, both in the Word of God, and our times spent in his presence listening for his voice. We are to continue to bathe in the loving words from our heavenly Daddy to each one of us. He just loves affirming us and telling us how special we are, and we are to constantly be filling ourselves up with his "life words."

Our connection daily to Jesus Christ gives us everything we need (John 15). As we stay connected to the vine daily, drinking from him, we will not be like those in the vision who wore the Jesus shirts. They said they knew Jesus, yet they feasted on things in their lives that did not glorify Jesus. They did not truly know the ever-continuing, deep revelation of his love, for how can one know the amazing love of God and not be transformed? By feasting on other things in their lives, they were kept from hearing the call of God in their lives.

If you are one who has been feasting upon worldly things while Jesus has been calling you to follow him, or you have been walking in complacency, do not doubt that Jesus loves you so much; He approves of you and He is here with you now with his arms outstretched. He has not a hint of condemnation in his heart. He is quietly calling you back to deep intimacy with him. He wants to show you how much He loves you, how special you are to him and to tell you of all the great plans He has for you and your life. All you have to do is turn around and walk into his arms through repentance. Come to Him in repentance, and He embraces you. He whispers His words of love over you again. He reminds you of what He purchased for you at Calvary and your identity in Him. You are righteous in Christ. You are washed by the blood of the Lamb. You are free. You are delighted in. Repentance is a beautiful word. It's making a change, a change of mind, an action. It's not going to God and begging and pleading for forgiveness. It's recognizing our wrong and aligning with His truth and changing our way. A beautiful realignment. As you repent for those things you have feasted on that have brought compromise, He will embrace you, and His love, comfort and words of life will fill you with peace, joy and your heart on fire for Him again.

Prayer:

Father, please forgive me for living in two worlds. Please forgive me for complacency in my life and for trying to serve two masters. I am sorry for not following hard after you and seeking you. Forgive me for feasting on things of this world. I ask that you wash me clean and ignite your fire in my heart again today. Break complacency and worldly ways out of my life in Jesus' name. Teach me to seek you and place a great hunger within me to know you more and feast deeply upon your Word. It is all or nothing I know, Lord, so I commit and surrender to you today. The cry of my heart now is, "Lord, I give it all to you and for you." In Jesus' name, amen.

Jesus loves you so much! His love for you does not change when you feast on things of this world. Yes, He is saddened, but He still loves you. He never condemns you, and He always wants the best for you. He desires that you come deeper into the knowledge of who He is, his never-ending amazing love for you and how to live completely for him. Feast, feast, feast upon his love for you and your intimacy with Jesus Christ daily!

1. Make time with him every day even if it is just five minutes to sit before him in stillness. Invest time in

getting to knowing him, and continue asking him to show you a deep revelation of how much He loves you and who you are to him, how amazingly wonderful and special you are!

2. Feast on his Word. You can do this through reading the Word, doing a study on a topic that interests you, or by memorizing Scripture.

3. Ask the Holy Spirit to open your ears, eyes, and heart to hear what He wants to speak to you through his Word.

It is time for us as Christians to live to the *fullest!* We should live out of the overflow of His love in our relationship with Jesus. Maintain your intimacy with him daily, be filled daily with his love again, and then give out and love others. Out of the overflow, ministry will occur. If you are empty spiritually, you will find yourself hindered in hearing his voice, ministering to others, and moving in the Spirit.

Prayer:
Father, I thank you that you have called me to follow after you. Please forgive me if in any way I have feasted on things not of you in my heart, my mind or my life. Lord, increase my hunger for you and for feasting on your Word. By the power of your Spirit, teach me to fight the good fight in my thought patterns and my everyday life.

I love you, Lord. I surrender to you again today. Have your way in my life. Continue to fuel my heart's fire for you that I may never walk in two worlds. Help me pursue you and take up my cross and follow you. Thank you for loving me. In Jesus' name, amen.

Ugly Unbelief

We know that the Word of God is full of authority. It is God-inspired (2 Timothy 3:16). We also know that his Word will never return to him void (Isaiah 55:11). What a guarantee we have there! God's Word will never return void. Even if we look at circumstances and do not see the outcome we expect, his Word will never fail. We cannot allow circumstances that didn't turn out the way we expected to change our understanding of the faithfulness of God, or the validity of His promises towards us. Whenever there is a disappointment in my life, or there is something I don't understand, the first thing I will do is invite the Holy Spirit to come in and minister to that area of disappointment or lack of understanding in my heart. Recognizing I don't have to understand, I just have to trust Him and still worship

Him in the mystery of it all, knowing that He is good and He is ALWAYS good. We have to guard our hearts from unbelief and invite Him to come and teach us His ways and increase our faith.

When we allow things to fester we can find that unbelief can take root and then our hearts proclaim that His Word *does* return void and it *does* fail. We do not believe because we have not yet seen; or we have seen, but we did not receive the answer we expected. We have to be very careful not to live with hearts full of unbelief.

Unbelief hinders our intimacy with Jesus, blinds our eyes to new revelations, and hardens our hearts to him and his love. It brings discouragement, depression, and oppression upon our lives. These are not the blessings from the heart of God for us. Ultimately, unbelief leads us away from Jesus. It definitely does nothing to draw us closer to him.

Unbelief also hinders our prayers. It negates them. It keeps healing from us. It keeps our blessings from us. It keeps the joy of the Lord from us. It takes away our peace. It creeps into every part of our lives, watering down our walk to nothing but formality and duty rather than life and relationship.

"Take care, brothers, lest there be in any of you an unbelieving heart, leading you to fall away from the living God." Hebrews 3:12 (cev)

Unbelief locks the Spirit and revelation out of our lives, and that is not the way to grow deeper in intimacy with Jesus. If we find our hearts full of unbelief, then we need to echo the cry of the man in Mark 9:24 who asked Jesus to help his unbelief.

This man's son was possessed with an evil spirit. The father told Jesus that it often threw him into the fire and into the water to kill him. Look at what the man said to Jesus in verse 22.

"If you can do anything, take pity on us and help us." Mark 9:22 (nasb)

Let's stop there for a moment. What do you see in that verse? There is that one little word that ushers in unbelief—*if!* Here the word *if* says to Jesus, "I am not sure you can, but I am willing to give you a go." That is not the kind of faith response Jesus wants. You see in verse 23, Jesus ministers directly to that unbelief.

"Jesus said to him, 'If you can? All things are possible to him who believes.'" Mark 9:23 (nasb)

Notice the very first words from Jesus "If you can?" Here Jesus is doing two things.

1. He is challenging the man's mindset of unbelief. "If you can?" I can imagine Jesus looking at this man with such love and saying something along the lines of "Do you really know who I am?"

2. Jesus highlighted the authority and power that the man had towards his own victory. Jesus said, "All things are possible *to him* who believes." Think how many opportunities we have missed breakthroughs because we have allowed our unbelief to shape our expectation and faith.

Look at part B of that verse, "All things are possible for him who believes." Now, think about that for a moment. Jesus was not saying all things are possible except for healing, financial provision, and freedom. No! Jesus said *all things* are possible for him who believes. Jesus does not lie, and I am sure you know that. Therefore, if the Word says something is true, then we need to kick unbelief out of our hearts. We already have assurance that God moves mountains and performs miraculous signs and wonders. He can work through all his people as long as they believe.

We combat any sort of unbelief in our hearts with the following cry. *"Lord, I do believe; help my unbelief." Mark 9:24 (nasb)*

Why do we so easily allow unbelief in our hearts? We oftentimes look through the wrong lenses. The lenses of this world are logical. They are not the lens of faith. Our lenses cause us to focus and view things. How do we view God's Word? How do we view God?

Jesus longs to do more within his bride than He is doing right now. Yes, He can do all things, but He chooses to move through us. We can sometimes slow the hand of God when we are not ready, where the "little foxes" of unbelief have hindered the harvest.

Look at Mark 9:14–19:

> *A large crowd was around them, and some scribes arguing with them. Immediately when the entire crowd saw him, they were amazed and began running to*

greet him. And He asked them, "What are you discussing with them?" and one of the crowd answered him, "Teacher I brought You my son, possessed with a spirit which makes him mute and whenever it seizes him, it slams him to the ground and he foams at the mouth, and grinds his teeth and stiffens out. I told your disciples to cast it out and they could not do it."

And He answered them and said, "O unbelieving generation, how long shall I be with you? How long shall I put up with you? Bring him to me." (nasb)

I believe that Jesus is now raising his church to a place where she will shine as she has never shone before. She will move in the power and authority that is *already hers*. We are not waiting for power or waiting for authority. It has already been given to us. If we are not moving in that power, then we need to examine ourselves for unbelief.

Yes, you may not see God answer you the way you desire, but He wants you to move in his power and authority. If you are not seeing that manifested in your life, please check your heart for unbelief.

Do you truly and honestly believe what Jesus said in Mark 9:23?

"Jesus said to him, 'If you can? All things are possible to him who believes.'" Mark 9:23 (nasb)

When we really take hold of that proclamation from the heart of Jesus, we are going to be a powerful universal church. Even now in some areas of the world, we see God do miraculous things. He is moving in great victory and authority, but there is a mentality of defeat in the church today. As Christians, we can walk in defeat and unbelief rather than in faith. This has been a real problem within the universal church today.

The body of Christ is now answering the call of the Lord to walk by faith (2 Corinthians 5:7), but our faith can be in unbelief rather than God.

It is easy to walk in fear of "What if I am wrong? What if it doesn't happen? What will people say if it doesn't turn out the way I believe?" Many do not believe that God can use them.

Many of us do not believe that this all authority and all power and all things are possible are for us, because we have a wrong view of God and his love and of ourselves. Our belief system often does not line up with what the Word says about us, so consequently our unbelief in the area of value and self-worth hinders God's work in us.

We must repent of those mindsets and replace the lies with the truth of who God says we are in the Word. We are chosen because of *his* work on the cross, not because of our works. God will use us because He loves us. We make ourselves available by believing who God says we are. We must be willing. Studying Scripture about how God loves us, values us, and will use us can help; meditating on it until it gets into our hearts. Unbelief in the area of self-worth hinders much of God's work through us. We need to deal with it.

By walking in this level of wrong faith and fear, we rob ourselves of the power and authority that Jesus desires for us.

"Truly, truly, I say to you, he who believes in me, the works that I

do, he will do also; and greater works than these he will do, because I go to the Father." John 14:12 (nasb)

Jesus was serious when He said that! As the universal body of Christ, we are to do greater works than He through the empowerment of the Holy Spirit.

It is time for us to rise up as a church and learn to take God at his Word. Even when things do not turn out how we expected, God's Word never ever changes. God is calling us now to:

1. Trust that He is who He says He is.

2. Trust that He will do what He says He will do.

3. Take time to check your heart and repent of any unbelief. Start taking risks on his Word, because He said, "All things are possible to him who believes."

What we believe must line up with his Word. It must not be taken out of context. It must follow the guidelines of Scripture. Let us shake off the things that hinder us and walk in victory, authority, and radical faith. We will now explore radical faith in the next chapter.

Church, it is time to shine! If you have seen unbelief in parts of your heart and life, let me lead you in a prayer of repentance. There is no condemnation for us in Christ Jesus (Romans 8:1), and I want to highlight here that if we do see areas of unbelief in our lives or areas where we fall short, we are not to allow even a hint of condemnation to come near us. Jesus knows exactly where we are at and our present struggles. It is our available heart to have his Spirit change us and rid us of unbelief that He delights in. Jesus does not expect perfection from us. He understands and allows our struggles and trials so our faith will be tested and take the place of our unbelief. He simply asks for a willing heart to change as the man cried out in Mark 9:24 (nasb) *"Lord I do believe; help my unbelief,"* and Jesus, being so loving, gracious, and compassionate, ministered to the man. So it is with us. He will meet us half way!

Father, please forgive me for my unbelief. I am sorry for not trusting you. I am sorry for not believing who you say you are. I am sorry that I have not believed what your Word says you will do.

Please forgive me and help my unbelief. Remove it from my life that it will not hinder my intimacy with you anymore. Unlock all the doors in my heart and life that have been locked by unbelief. Unlock every door that has kept you out. Come into my life in those areas that you have now unlocked, Lord. Have your perfect will in my life.

Teach me to rise up in faith that all things are possible to him who believes.

Thank you, Lord, for your love, your forgiveness, and the privilege that we have to walk in great power and authority because of Jesus' death and resurrection at Calvary. In Jesus' name, amen.

If you prayed that prayer for forgiveness, Jesus forgives you. Today is a new day to walk forward taking Jesus at his Word as you never have before. Keep asking the Lord to open the ears and eyes of your heart to hear his Word, see more of his love, and then move forward.

When unbelief is broken from your life, you will experience wonderful blessings and freedom. I have struggled with unbelief in the area of my identity. I understand and see so clearly how it hinders our walk with the Lord. It prevents us from growing in him and holds us down. Walking the road of freedom from unbelief is very exciting. That freedom gives a person revelation, peace, and joy in the Holy Spirit. God's love for us is incredible, and as we see more and more of his love in our lives and hold onto truth, walking by faith, unbelief will fall away.

The Lord placed a word on my heart for his bride that encapsulates the theme of this chapter.

"Take care, brothers, lest there be in any of you an unbelieving heart, leading you to fall away from the living God." Hebrews 3:12 (esv)

Unbelieving Hearts

My precious church, I am calling you to examine your hearts in the light of my presence. I am moving in many lives and many hearts. I am seeking to cause each of you to grow, to strengthen each of you, and to build you into strong pillars for me.

Beware of unbelieving hearts, my church. The enemy has come to steal, kill, and destroy. Many of you wonder why you are being so hammered by the enemy. I say unto you, examine your hearts to make sure that there are no seeds of unbelief within them. Many of you look at my Word and long to see the manifestations of my promise come to life in your hearts and lives. You wonder why they do not come to pass. My church, keep your eyes open and examine your hearts for seeds of unbelief that could take you out of the position to receive.

Many of you feel oppression and strong discouragement over your lives. It is because you allow lies the enemy offers you to enter your hearts. It opens the door for him to bring the fruit of his kingdom into your lives. Do not listen to the lies the enemy throws at you.

My Word will get each of you through this hard time and dark valley. Holding closely and tightly to my promises will bring a greater manifestation of my heart, my promises and my glory into your lives.

Come before me in repentance and lay down your unbelief. To walk in unbelief, my church, is to have a skewed view of who I am. I am calling you to come to me and repent for your unbelief so that I may cleanse you and set you free.

I love you with an everlasting love and desire to continue to mold you into all that I have created you to be, my Bride. Now is the time to take my Word and look at it with the eyes of your hearts open. Decide to take my Word wholeheartedly. Do not just take little bites, but fill your hearts with my Words of truth. Allow the truth of my Word and your repentance to wash away unbelief once and for all.

I am drawing a line in the sand, my church. Come and count the cost. Surrender your lives to me. Surrender all you have and take a stand for the truth of my Word. As you do this, my church, you will see the mighty moves of my Spirit for which many of you are crying out.

No longer allow your unbelief to keep me out of areas of your hearts, your lives, and your congregations. I desire to lavish my love upon you as you have never seen before. I desire to pour out my Spirit in greater measure and reveal my heart and loving-kindness within your midst.

The line has been drawn. No more unbelief; instead we have radical revelatory love, truth, and…

Radical faith!

Radical Faith

Do you know that we are called to walk in deep levels of radical faith? Really, we are, it says it right here:

"Jesus told them. 'For truly I say to you, if you have faith like a grain of mustard seed, you will say to this mountain, "Move from here to there" and it will move, and nothing will be impossible for you.'" *Matthew 17:20* (esv)

Faith as small as a mustard seed—have you ever seen a mustard seed? It is small and does not really amount to much. Yet we see in this verse that Jesus says we could say to this mountain, "Move from here to there," and it would move. Look at those words at the end: "Nothing would be impossible." That is a huge statement to make.

What we need to recognize and take into consideration when we look at this verse is that nothing is impossible for us when we align ourselves with the promises of God.

"Delight yourself in the Lord and He will give you the desires of your heart." Psalm 37:4 (esv)

Faith is a difficult challenge to us sometimes, isn't it? God will allow circumstances to come into our lives to test our faith. He really wants to challenge us to believe wholeheartedly the promises contained within his Word. God indeed does and will give us the rightful desires of our hearts as we align our hearts with his Word.

The Bible is full of God's promises for us. He longs to lavish good things upon us (Matthew 7:11). His heart is ready and waiting to pour out his goodness on us. All that we will ever need we have in Christ. The key to walking in the manifestations of these promises is faith. We do not know how long we will wait till the manifestation occurs, or how God will choose to act upon his Word, but as we activate faith in our hearts, we will grow more and more in receiving the promises that He has for us contained in his Word.

Do you know what is interesting? We already have everything we need in him, yet we can choose not to walk in it by not walking in faith. That is a scary concept, eh? I have already touched on this subject in previous chapters, but I am recapping them because they are crucial to our intimacy with Jesus.

We cannot walk in a deep, intimate relationship with Jesus if we are not being constantly stretched, challenged, and purged in the area of our faith. In the Western world, we have become so distracted by material possessions that we are very reliant upon them. When material possessions disappear, we jump on the worry wagon, and it is then we see what is truly in our hearts.

I write this with tremendous conviction and humility because this is the very path that I am now walking. As I write this chapter, I have stepped out in faith and left my job of four years. Jesus told me through the strongest feeling of conviction within my heart to do this and be like Abram. I do not know where I am going or what is next. It definitely does bring up questions like, "Lord, how are we going to survive on one income? Lord, how are we going to pay all the bills? Lord, I am discouraged because I do not know what is next for me!"

Do you know what Jesus said to me? He said, "Lana, I love you more than you can ever dream, think, or imagine, so where I guide you, I will provide. You must see in your questions that a lack of faith still remains within your heart." Talk about gentle loving conviction, yet an encouragement! Ouch! The Lord is always looking on the earth to find those who walk in deep faith with him. God knows we're not perfect, nor expects it, but He does expect a willing and available heart to be transformed by his Spirit. You know what really gets God's attention? *Faith!* Faith can be understood as knowing in our own power and strength we can accomplish nothing, but in Christ all things are possible. God loves to see his people walk in faith despite their circumstances. When we are faced with situations such as this, any circumstance that requires faith (which are so many in everyday life, aren't they?!), and the questions start flooding us, this is the time we must stand up in faith no matter what the outcome, know He loves us incredibly and wants only good for us, and begin to proclaim the promises of God.

Jesus is building a church of people who walk in radical faith. What do I mean by radical faith? It is faith that is not afraid to *dream*. It is faith that is not afraid to *go against* the logical boundaries of our minds. It is faith that knows Jesus loves them incredibly, always works for their good, and wants what's best for them. It is faith that is ready to take a risk and believe wholeheartedly through the empowerment of the Holy Spirit that mountains *can* and *will* be moved in his name.

It is all about Jesus' name. It is not the way we proclaim it or how loud we scream it. It has nothing to do with us. It is all about Jesus, his love, his power, and his authority. It is about the privilege He gave us to carry his power and authority, which was achieved for us through his death and resurrection.

We see throughout history men and women who rose up in radical faith. Because of them lives and nations changed when they took the Word of God and ran with it. They did not give up until they saw the manifestation of what was already theirs. Because of their faith the promises came to fruition in their lives. Why could those men and women who rose up in radical faith never give up? Certainly, because the Holy Spirit empowered them, but also because they *knew* how much their Daddy loved them! Knowing Daddy's love is the foundation of *so* much in our lives and is an essential foundation for moving forward in radical faith.

God is raising forerunners right now. These are called to walk in greater levels of revelation of Daddy's love and of radical faith. They will meet situations that require faith that they have not known before. It will require that they walk in

humility as examples to the body of Christ. As they do this, they will lead the church to greater degrees of radical faith.

"For we walk by faith, not by sight." 2 Corinthians 5:7 (nasb) The great challenge of this verse echoes throughout history in the Christian world. It is echoing in the heart of God today. As we walk in a deep revelation of his love and walk by faith and not by sight, we walk in a deep level of trust that Jesus Christ is who He says He is. When you know the great love someone has for you, you trust them. If we had a full revelation of our Daddy's love, we would never doubt, would we? We walk by faith rooted in love. Doing this will propel us into deeper intimacy with him. The more we see him, the more we will trust. The more we trust him, the more we see of him It is amazing the way that He has set everything up for us so perfectly. As we continue to delight in knowing him and his love, we will walk in obedience down the path He has already paved for us. What an awesome God we serve!

One who walks in deep radical faith is one who proclaims the truths of God's amazing love and promises despite his circumstances. That person chooses to put on the garment of praise no matter what. Walking in these principles from God's Word (knowing his love, proclaiming the truth, and wearing the garment of praise) will propel us into the call of God to walk in radical faith.

Terrible or Terrific Tongue

"My dear friends, with our tongues we speak both praises and curses. We praise our Lord and Father, and we curse people who were created to be like God, and this isn't right. Can clean water and dirty water both flow from the same spring?" James 3:9–11 (cev)

The tongue is so powerful. It has the power to uplift or tear down in a second. Have you ever had someone you trusted or even someone that you do not really know say something hurtful to you? No matter who they were to you, it still hurt. Words hurt a lot.

The old childhood saying, "Sticks and stones may break my bones, but words will never hurt me" is not an accurate saying. Think about how others have shattered people by saying something cruel to them. People turn away from God because a member of the congregation spoke something unkind to them. Families are torn apart, marriages broken, friendships crushed because of the power of the spoken word.

Words also have a positive side. We all know how good it is when someone encourages us or tells us that we did a good job. It is nice to hear that someone really appreciates or loves you. How beautiful is it to read God's words of love and promises to us in the Word? We are brought comfort and strength, aren't we? We as humans are very blessed by encouraging, loving words.

People really bless us when they speak good, loving, life-giving words over us. God created us to give and to receive excellent, loving words. God wants all of us to spread his love and blessings through words we speak over others.

In the first chapters of Genesis, we see that God spoke everything into existence. His spoken word was very powerful. Because God made us in his image, our spoken words are also very powerful. James warns us to pay attention to the power of our tongue.

"And the tongue is a fire, a world of unrighteousness. The tongue is set among our members, staining the whole body, setting on fire the entire course of life, and set on fire by hell. For every kind of beast and bird, of reptile and sea creature, can be tamed and has been tamed by mankind, but no human being can tame the tongue. It is a restless evil, full of deadly poison." James 3:6–8 (esv)

Jesus showed me that what we speak aligns us with either the kingdom of heaven or the kingdom of darkness. It is up to us to choose which one we want. Whatever thoughts we entertain and whatever words we speak will open God's "door" or the enemy's "door" over our lives. The choice is ours! Our words create; what you speak is what you will get.

To walk in deeper levels of radical faith defies our circumstances with power-filled, Holy Spirit-saturated words of truth. Those words speak reality into our circumstances. The physical realm is not reality. Reality is what the Word of God says and what we choose to confess.

So, in my stepping out of my job into the unknown

where finances and ministry are not certain, I must continue to delight in his love for me and how He has all good things for me (Luke 11:13) and proclaim the truth of God's Word. The proclamation is *"Seek first the kingdom of God and his righteousness and all these things will be added to you. Therefore, do not be anxious about tomorrow, for tomorrow will be anxious about itself, sufficient for the day is its own trouble"* (Matthew 6:33–34, esv).

This is the answer to my situation! In this verse is the truth of my circumstance. I do not know the next step. I do not see from where finances will flow. I do not know what tomorrow will bring. None of that matters because reality says as I seek first the Kingdom of God, God will give me everything else I need. I do not need to worry because He loves me and will provide all I need because He adores me! Same goes for you and the rest of his children! My responsibility in this situation is to use my tongue to proclaim those words above that are truth.

Now, sometimes when I speak those words, my emotions and heart do not believe it. However, do you know what the key is when it comes to using your tongue? It is a choice! Speak out the Word of God constantly and your emotions will end up following your confession of faith.

Going deeper in intimacy and love with Jesus and hearing his voice depends upon what you speak out of your mouth. If you speak negative statements over your life, your spouse, your family, your situations, and your friends, you are going to sow bad seeds into your life and their lives and reap the fruit of those bad seeds.

They will hinder you from growing in the revelation of who Jesus is and his love. They will stop you from hearing his voice and knowing his heart. We are not to walk around in fear all the time being scared of what we say. When we do speak bad words, if we repent, we must know we are forgiven, and as we speak out the right words, from God's Word, He will honor our obedience.

Be careful when you use your tongue to speak things contrary to the Word of God. If you choose to allow your circumstances to dictate what you are feeling and proclaiming, you are ultimately saying that your feelings and your circumstances have more weight than the Word of God. We know that this is not the case.

You also may be questioning whether the Lord has the right to interfere with your life. Some Christians get angry with the Lord when He does not do what they want. They treat Jesus as their genie, *not* their *Lord*.

Faith in the Lord means that we have *faith* in the best way he leads us for our lives. After all he loves you more than anyone else ever has or will, and his love is pure and eternal. So, with that kind of love, the best Daddy around; wouldn't he want to give you what is best? Of course! Even if we don't get what we "think" we need, believe me, we will get better than we expected (Ephesians 3:20). We cannot see and know all things, but the Lord is all-seeing and all-knowing. He does not need our direction. We must allow him to direct our steps, hence we walk by faith.

God has given us a tremendous privilege to walk in deep levels of radical faith. He allows us to see mountains moved through our confession. We use the tongues that God gave us to proclaim his truths.

Do you see his Word as a reality despite what your circumstances say? Do you allow your circumstances to fill your heart with more worry than faith? God is looking for those forerunners who will walk the deep levels of faith. Be ready, though, when you are ready to walk there; God may propel you into a circumstance that will really leave you no option than to trust Him. Keep your mouth full of His decrees. What is He saying? Keep decreeing before you see it. After all that is what it means to walk by faith and not by sight, right? Like Elijah in 2 Kings, he "heard the sound of rain" before the cloud the size of a man's hand had risen out of the sea. Elijah positioned himself and decreed and interceded, based upon what God had spoken, before it became a reality. Elijah's reality was what HE said, not the natural circumstances around him. We can learn so much from this very beautiful example in Elijah's life of aligning ourselves with the reality of heaven, what God is speaking, engaging with it, and decreeing it, until we see what God has spoken, manifested.

What door do you open with your words over your life and the lives of others? Are you ushering in the blessings of God and more of his Spirit by proclaiming his promises contained in the Word of God? Could you possibly give the enemy a huge open door to heap all of his junk on you? Do you entertain worry, doubt, fear, anxiety, condemnation, or guilt?

Let us watch our tongues! We have the power to lift

up and tear down! To walk in radical faith, we need terrific tongues of blessing, not terrible tongues of curses.

If we speak negative, harmful, discouraging words over our lives or the lives of others, we should humble ourselves before God in repentance. We can then ask Him to teach us to speak His promises and His blessings instead. God gives us the power to do that through the Holy Spirit. We have already overcome because of the shed blood of Jesus, and what a privilege it is that He gave us such power in our words. God really trusts us!

It is no coincidence that in Matthew 17:20 Jesus says, "*Say* to this mountain move, and it will be moved," because one of the most powerful tools we have been given is the proclamation from our mouths. Let us have guards over our mouths to speak only what He desires for us and not allow the flesh, other people, or the enemy to lead us to speak things contrary to God's Word.

As we speak out his promises, we will grow in a faith that we have never experienced before. Romans 10:17 says that faith comes through hearing the Word of God. Yes, it comes through hearing it preached, taught, and our own mouths proclaiming it over our own lives. God's promises for us are encouraging, uplifting and full of faith. We just need to tap into them!

Purposeful Praise

To walk in radical faith, we are to be people who walk in purposeful praise. No matter what we are facing in our circumstances, we are to praise his holy name. Our circumstances change and our lives change, but Jesus never changes (Hebrews 13:8).

Jesus is worthy of all our praise today and forever. If Jesus never did anything else for us but die for us, forgive our sins, and guarantee us eternal life for accepting him it would be more than enough reason to praise his holy name forever. His love is so beautiful, so pure, so magnificent; He is so worthy of praise. Anything else Jesus does for us is an added bonus to the greatest gift of all: his love and salvation.

In each of our lives, we walk through times of heaviness; times of sadness, hardship, trial, confusion, discouragement, grief, but despite our circumstances, we are to praise his name. Isaiah 61:3 says to put on a garment of praise in exchange for the spirit of heaviness. We are never to take off that garment of praise. It is a garment to wear at all times.

The past year I worked a job I did not enjoy anymore. I found myself very unhappy to remain in that position. I felt the uneasiness of being in the same place for a long t i m e , craving a new challenge, yet every time I took my feelings to Jesus, He comforted me and then quietly challenged me about praising him despite my circumstances. Although my surroundings were not what I wanted at the time, He had not changed. I served him simply by being in that place.

Through that season, Jesus reminded me of the following verse:

"Through him, therefore let us constantly and at all times offer up

to God a sacrifice of praise; which is the fruit of our lips and thankfully acknowledge and confess and glorify his name." Hebrews 13:15

A sacrifice of praise! That is exactly what it is when we are in difficult circumstances. When the last thing we would think of doing is praising his name, this is the very thing we need to do. That is why it is a sacrifice. We may not feel like doing it. We may not understand why we are to keep praising his name when things are so bad.

When we do not see things manifest as we thought they would, that is when we see our focus has shifted. As long as Jesus Christ is our focus, nothing in our circumstances will keep us from praising him. He never changes, and He is worthy of all praise. People who walk in radical faith are people who purposefully praise him.

Chains break, heaviness lifts, oppression shatters, the enemy runs away and discouragement disappears when we praise his name. The floodgates of heaven open and his Spirit falls. Jeremiah 23:29 says, "'Is not My Word like fire' declares the Lord 'and like a hammer that breaks a rock in pieces.'" It is his Spirit working through his Word in our lives that sets us free.

When we worship in Spirit and in truth (John 4:24), the presence of God will manifest in our surroundings because we make room for him. Testify to his goodness, and to the wonderful name of Jesus Christ, and we find the Spirit present in our praise. Never stop praising; never stop rejoicing! (Philippians 4:4)

Purposeful praisers! That is what He calls us to be!

Jesus Christ never changes, so our praise to him should never end.

Below is a word that the Lord gave me in 2007, a word that is a truth on God's heart continually. He looks for radical people who will rise up in faith and believe his Word as complete truth, powerful, God-breathed, and full of authority. He wants us to take that truth and see our lives changed as we proclaim it over our lives.

Faith Arises Word

Many of you find yourselves in circumstances in the physical realm where the process and the journey seems long. The problem appears too big, and the mountain too large. However, I speak to you, my church, that this is where I am teaching you to walk by faith.

For situations and circumstances that seem impossible, I speak to you now that the answer is my Word. The answer to your healing, to your financial issues, and to your deliverance is all within my Word. The answer to your freedom, to your hope, to your joy, to your guidance, and to your direction is all within my Word.

I am releasing those of my children who are walking hard roads. Through those hard roads you have learnt one of the greatest lessons of all: that my Word is living. My Word is alive, and my Word is the Sword that breaks through all things. My church, you do not use the Word as much as you could.

You have the power contained within my Word to change lives, situations, nations, and the world. I send this Word of mine through your speech. I anoint many tongues that do not speak. I call you, my church, to invite heaven to earth and walk in your inheritance in ways greater than you ever have. Raise your proclamation of my Word.

My church, I love you all so much. I love you with an everlasting love, a love that you can never truly understand. It is a love that caused me to give the greatest sacrifice so that you may be free and live in relationship with me. I encourage you, my church, to search your hearts. Search your hearts in the light of my presence. If you find any unbelief of my Word, repent and allow me to uproot it and remove it completely.

Many of you cry out for change and breakthrough in your lives and the lives of others. However, I tell you, my church, speak out my Word. Speak out the answer, and my Spirit will move as I send my Word forth.

I am now increasing the hunger for my Word within many hearts. I am showing many the importance of my Word. Now is the time, my church, to have your words ready and sharp so that you may use one of the greatest gifts I have given you; my Word!

Now is the time to step up to the battle line. I am looking for those who are willing to rise up and those who are desperate for the manifestation of my written Word. I look for those who are hungry to see their spiritual inheritance. They want me to give to them full measure in their everyday lives of that which is already theirs.

My church, I am ready to lavish all things upon you that I have already paid for at Calvary. You may access all these great riches through the power of the proclamation of my written Word. Rise up in faith in a way you never have before. Do not look at your circumstances.

The latter rain of my Spirit is falling upon those who are calling it down. Those who are hungry for the rain of my Spirit will receive. Do not stay under the shelter of habit where you are comfortable. Step out and rise up in faith knowing that my Word will always come to pass. The rain of my Spirit will fall on you as you have never ever seen before.

I love you, my church, arise those of you who are willing to have my Word burn in your hearts as they never have before.

Prayer: Father, I thank you that through Jesus we receive all blessing and truth. Thank you that through the death and resurrection of your Son, Jesus, we have eternal life when we choose to follow him. Father, I thank you that you call us to rise up in radical faith. Thank you that we do not have to be afraid to proclaim your Word. Thank you for all you have done for us. Forgive me for walking in doubt and unbelief or for speaking curses with my tongue. Lord, teach me to tame my tongue, to believe wholeheartedly, and to claim your Word. Teach me to choose to praise always. Send me forth to new levels of faith. I am willing, Lord. In Jesus' name, amen.

Passionately Pursuing His Presence

The American Heritage® Dictionary (2009) defines pursuit as

1. To chase.

2. To strive.

From the beginning of time God has passionately pursued us as his creation. It was out of his passionate love for us that He chose to create us in his image (Genesis 1:26). God is so passionate. He is passionate about his kingdom, his work, and his creation—*us*! He is the epitome of passion. **S**adly, there are many who are not yet able to experience the reality that God loves and enjoys them. There are those who argue that God could not possibly love them. What a person believes about

God is the most important thing they think. It affects everything they do.

For too many Christians, God seems remote, impersonal, and unknowable. Because of that, many suffer from an inability to feel forgiven. They are nagged by doubt and condemnation and do not know that God loves them.

When I say that God passionately loves us, it is an agape love.

Agape love is defined by American Psychological Association as:

1. The love of God or Christ for humankind.

2. The love of Christians for other persons, corresponding to the love of God for humankind.

3. Unselfish love of one person for another without sexual implications; brotherly love.

Agape love comes from God. It is a love that does not demand or expect anything in return. It is pure, unselfish, and holy. How do we get full of his agape love? Keep asking him to fill us up (Romans 5:5).

The word passion in the world today can have connotations that I do not attribute to God. The passion within this chapter is that same passion in God's heart. It is pure, holy, and full of agape love. Pure, holy, godly passion rooted in agape love is passion that consistently calls us to action. That action is often radical action.

As we are made in the image of God, we reflect his

love to others. We do not have the power or the strength to love as He loves. We allow his love and his strength to flow through us to touch the lives of others.

So, what is God's passion?

Genesis 1:27 says God created Adam and said it was very good. Jeremiah 1:5 says that He created and formed you and knew you from your mother's womb. Jeremiah 29:11 says that He has called you and given you a plan and a purpose; He has good plans for *you.* John 10:10 says that Jesus wants you to live abundantly. Second Corinthians 5:21 says that in Christ you are the righteousness of God; Galatians 4:7 says that you are a joint heir with Christ and much more. Do you see the common thought in all those verses?

You! God is passionate about you!

God is extremely passionate about *the relationship* you have with him. He sent Jesus so that we can be friends with God. We need to be constantly developing our relationship with God. We need to become intimate friends with God as Moses was. Why wouldn't we want to develop a relationship with the one who loves us more than anyone has ever loved us or ever will, and who will never work for our harm always bring the best out of everything?

Jesus' first passion was his relationship with his Father. He constantly listened to the Father's heart. After that He continually obeyed the Father's commands. Jesus' priority was having a relationship with his Father and with us. He only did that which He saw the Father doing (John 5:19). What do we see within the Trinity? We see a relationship between Father, Son, and Spirit. Relationship is on the heart of God. Relationship is a passion that God wants to develop within the hearts of every believer.

We are called to be passionate pursuers of his presence and his heart. Before anything else in our Christian lives, we must passionately pursue his presence. It is in seeing his love for us, his heart and learning who He is that we grow and are transformed in his image. Before evangelizing, before ministering, before anything else, we are to passionately pursue his presence. We do not pursue his presence because He is out of reach or because He plays hide and seek with us. We pursue him out of hunger and desperation.

We cannot drive our cars unless we fill them with petrol (gasoline). It is the same with us. We must first and foremost pursue Jesus and his heart. Then we are fueled with his great love for us, others, and his Spirit and overflow to give out to others.

Fabulous programs do not draw people into the church to know Jesus not nearly as much as the testimony and example and love of people who are passionately pursuing Jesus. Those passionately in love with him will change the lives of others.

Much of the universal church is asleep today. We are not awake to all God is doing. We are not awake to his great love and call upon our lives. God wants his church to wake up! He wants us to arise and see and grow in his deep love for us day by day and receive all that He has for us. Most of all He wants us to passionately pursue intimacy with him.

Now do we know what our number one passion

should be? It is *Jesus* and our relationship with him first. We are called to passionately pursue his presence. No matter what we do in life; no matter where we are; we must welcome his presence into our everyday lives. Our second passion should be our relationship with others and our ministry.

How?

1. *We grow in passion for him in times set aside specifically for him.* Here we know him and his love and grow in listening to him.

2. *Invite in his presence.* At work, at home, in the grocery store, no matter where we are we invite his presence into our lives. His presence will lead us, guide us, and use us. Inviting his presence into any situation will automatically change the atmosphere of a workplace, environment, or situation.

It is oftentimes hard to pursue him at work because we are so busy. We do not have time to do anything except hope that soon the wave of craziness will end. When I worked, I asked Jesus how to be a passionate pursuer all the time. I heard him say, "Keep inviting me in." He is always with us, but when we invite him in we surrender and let *him* have full control.

With his help, I trained myself to invite his presence into
my current situation no matter what I was doing. Things really changed. I found myself more peaceful,

more loving, and more gracious. The fire to know him more burned brighter inside of me the more I invited him.

We cannot conjure up passion for Jesus Christ or wish it into being. Passion and intimacy with him go hand in hand. The more we spend time with him, knowing him and his great love for us, the more passionate we will be to know his heart. His presence will rest on our lives like never before. We need to be with Jesus. Quietly, we must sit in his presence, continue to invite his love deeper into our hearts, read his Word, and worship. Only then will a passion for him rise up within us as the Holy Spirit touches our hearts.

If we do not feel we are receiving passion even though we ask God to ignite more in us, we must ask him if anything hinders that passion. Things that can squash our passion for Jesus are:

1. Unforgiveness toward another person

2. Not spending time with him

3. Not being in his Word

4. Unrepented sin

5. Disobedience.

He will show us if there is anything in the way. He does not want to leave us where we are. He wants us free, so he will show us anything hindering us. He also shows us how to deal with things that are wrong.

Repentance is always the key! When we repent of anything hindering our walk with him, we open the door to freedom.

Intimacy with Jesus Christ is the essence of our Christian existence. It is all about our growing more mature as passionate pursuers of his heart. We must know who he is and walk in his presence. Intimacy propels us into greater levels of joy.

As we learn daily to invite his presence into all our situations, we see his presence change everything about us. It changes the way we serve and the way we treat others.

God calls us to be desperate to be in his presence. Here

is someone who was desperate to be in the presence of Jesus because she knew exactly who he was.

And Jesus rose and followed him, with his disciples. And behold, a woman who had suffered from a discharge of blood for twelve years came up behind him and touched the fringe of his garment, for she said to herself, "If I only touch his garment, I will be made well." Jesus turned, and seeing her he said, "Take heart, daughter; your faith has made you well." And instantly the woman was made well. Matthew 9:19–22 (esv)

This woman made Jesus her first priority. She forsook everything else. She did not care what people thought or how she looked. She just moved forward in desperation toward the one who mattered most to her. Yes, she wanted healing, however, she knew when she encountered Jesus that he would change her. Her desperation was met with a response of love, encouragement, and acceptance from Jesus. *"Daughter, your faith has made you well" (verse 22).*

She already *knew* who he was, and she *knew* his power.

She knew that if she just moved forward into his presence, he would heal her and change her forever. Imagine how she felt after he healed her! She probably experienced desperation to be in his presence even more. It is the same with us. If we are desperate to encounter Jesus, the hungrier we are each time we come close to him.

This lady was an outcast in society because of her illness. However, she was someone who had determination and desperation. These are the two things needed to be a passionate pursuer of Christ.

In previous chapters, we have already addressed hungering, thirsting, and being desperate for Jesus. In this chapter, I would like to address determination.

Determination

Means the quality of mind which reaches definite conclusions.

Decision of character, or resoluteness.

We must determine in our hearts *daily* that Jesus is our passion. He is our life. We live, move, and breathe in him, and we must determine to seek him above all else.

We determine to set our faces toward God like a flint so that we may walk in deeper intimacy with him. Yes, we see people like Charles Spurgeon or Smith

Wigglesworth who spent hours in prayer seeking God, and that is wonderful, but sometimes that is not a doable thing for some of us with our lifestyles. We simply find it hard sitting still for so long. Our minds wander.

God wants his people to determine to be people of *priority!* God calls us to prioritize our time with him in our daily lives.

What does prioritizing Jesus mean to you?

Do you know how American Heritage Dictionary, 2009, defines to prioritize?

1. To choose what is most important to you.

2. To arrange or do in order of importance; give all of yourself to this cause.

3. To organize or deal with something according to its importance.

We will invest much of our time in something that is our priority, something we greatly love. We will expend our effort, our money and our lives for it because it is the most important thing to us.

Jesus Christ is to be our priority. He is the most important thing in our lives. Where do we prioritize Jesus in our lives? Are we passionately pursuing him by placing him at the top of the list no matter what we are doing?

Jesus spoke to me about putting him number one in all things. I said confidently, "Of course, Lord, I put you first, above all."

Then he said to me, "Even above your sleep?"

I responded, "Of course, Lord, you are more important to me than sleep." (I had no idea what I was getting myself into.)

The Lord then said, "Okay, Lana, I want you to get up every morning at five a.m. to spend time just seeking me."

Ouch!

I thought I would respond with, "Of course, Lord. I will happily do that!" Although my response was obedient, let me tell you, there was a part of me that almost died! "Ah, Lord, I need my sleep." I am not a morning person, so I do not do well in the mornings. At that moment, I felt the Lord pose this question to my heart, *"How desperate are you for me? How determined are you to pursue me and know me?"*

That question forever changed my life. That question

changed my thinking, governed my decision making, and opened my eyes to see how desperate God wants us to be for him. A great truth that really hit me in those times was; because he loves you and I so much, he is desperate to spend time with us too. He delights in us and loves us making time to sit with him. He enjoys us just as much as we enjoy him.

God asks Christians to set aside all other loves. Anything with greater importance than Jesus is an idol. Having an idol is a sin. God wants to be our first priority in everything. We must determine to spend more time in his presence.

How are your quiet times? How is your personal time of reading the Word? How is your worship? How is your intimacy with Jesus? Are you receiving more revelation of his amazing love for you? Are you prioritizing your time with him above all else? What circumstance in your life takes priority over Jesus? As we want him more, he will manifest himself to us in unimaginable ways. These questions are not to set "rules" to have a "religious relationship" with Jesus, to "do the right things" to be accepted by him. You are already accepted by him because of his death and resurrection; he loves you unconditionally. These questions are a gauge to determine how healthy your relationship with Jesus is right now. Some questions:

1. *Have you lost your passion for Jesus?*

2. *Are you not pursuing his presence and growing in intimacy with him?*

3. *Are you struggling in your quiet time with him?*

4. *Is there something holding you back from knowing him?*

5. *Do you need to sacrifice something in your life to him?*

No matter where you are, Jesus wants you to pursue him as never before. Get into his Word more, spend time worshipping Him. Surrender to Him daily. Come to God to reflect on his beauty and take your desires to Him. Passionately pursue Him now, and let his Spirit minister to you.

I hope that the following words will encourage and

challenge you. They are the constant cry of God's heart.

Intimacy Vision

I saw myself in a crowded hall, and people were dancing everywhere. I watched these people dance. As I looked upon each individual person, I saw they were dancing with Jesus. One at a time, yet all were dancing closely with Him. I knew I was seeing into a supernatural realm. I could see all these people individually dancing with Jesus, yet there was only one Jesus.

As they were dancing, they were not touching. Their arms were not around each other. No part of their physical bodies touched, yet they moved in perfect unison with Jesus.

I thought to myself, *how are they staying so close to Him and so united with Him if they are not holding onto Him?*

The Spirit showed me what was happening. As I looked closely, I saw their hearts held them close to Jesus. Each person's heart was intertwined with Jesus' heart. It formed a strong, thick bond that held them together firmly.

I heard the Spirit say that when one pulls away from Jesus, it not only damages their heart but it damages his heart. It creates a grieving pain of lost connection and lost intimacy. Jesus desires for his church to be dancing with Him, heart to heart, never pulling away. He always pulls us closer by the tug of his heart. As the bride passionately pursues Him and his presence, their hearts will be intertwined with his as they have never known.

Then I believe the Lord spoke the following word:

Passionate Pursuers of His Presence—
Arise! My church, I am calling you to come to dance with me. Allow me to draw you closer. Allow me to show you that through our being connected heart to heart, I can draw you to the place you need to be. Rise up in passionate pursuit of me and my presence, and we will be connected deeper and deeper.

Heart to heart, I speak of intimacy. I desire my church to know my heart so well. I desire that she know the very beat of my heart and what my heart is speaking. I want my church to know what my heart is feeling and know what my heart is releasing.

Church, I have called you to be my friends, not slaves. I am so passionate about you, my bride. I call you my chosen vessels, my glorious bride. I do not call you my slaves to carry out all my desires.

I call you friends, because I long to share my heart with you. I long to give to you the love that drove me to the cross. I long to reveal to you the very secrets of my heart and kingdom keys. They are all within my heart. Come passionately pursue my presence and my heart.

My bride, I bring you to a place of purifying, a place of cleansing, and a place of deeper intimacy. It is a place where your passion for my name will grow as you have never known before. It is a place where you will truly know my heart.

Many do not walk closely with me. Many hold onto my name but do not know my heart.

They do not passionately pursue my presence or my heart. Many carry my banner in their everyday lives but do not know my heart. Their passion to know me has died. This grieves me greatly.

I, the Lord your God, have called you to be my friends. I have called you to be hearers of my heart, passionate pursuers of my presence. Those who do not hear my heart will not prosper in the things to which I have called them.

Many cry out that they do not know how to hear my heart. I speak to you to hear my heart through my Word and reflective prayer. I will release you into all areas that I am calling you.

Many ministering now know my heart and are close to me. To those I speak that you continue to seek me. Continue to listen to my heart, and I shall enlarge your tent pegs. You will increase.

My church, you are called to be my friends. Will you sacrifice all things of your flesh, and of this world? Will you shake off all things that hold you down and come to me? Will you allow me to connect us heart to heart in a way you have never known? Passionately pursue me, and my presence and I will always be found by you. Rise up in passion for my name.

I, the Lord your God, am waiting, church. Arise!

Prayer:

Father, in Jesus' name, I thank you that you have called me as your own. Thank you that you are so passionate about who I am and the call you have placed on my life.

Thank you that your passion for me stems from your agape love for me. Lord, continue to ignite the passion within my heart to pursue you as I never have before.

Please forgive me for any ways I have squashed my passion for your heart and your name. Teach me to be a person who chooses you above all else and glorifies your name in all I do. In Jesus' name, amen.

Learning to Listen

There is one thing that I have learnt over the past few years walking with Jesus—*his desire to speak to us is greater than our desire to listen.* Jesus longs for his bride to have her ear continually planted upon his chest, hearing his heartbeat. We are to continue to learn and follow his direction at all times. At the outset of this chapter, I just want to highlight that not all of us are going to hear God in the same way. Not all of us are going to have visions, or dreams. You may hear God clearly through worship or through his Word. God may choose to speak to you through different ways all the time. It is not wrong to desire to hear God in deeper and different ways. If you pray and seek Him to speak to you, he will answer. Keep hungering to hear Him; never stop asking Him to broaden the way you hear his voice. It is amazing the creativity of our God in the way he chooses to communicate with us.

Jesus is molding his bride into the manifestation of John 5:19 (esv):

"So Jesus said to them, 'Truly, truly, I say to you, the Son can do nothing of his own accord, but only what he sees the Father doing. For whatever the Father does, that the Son does likewise.'"

In this hour Jesus is raising up his bride to where he has called her to be. The Spirit of God is calling out to his church to *hear what the Spirit says to the churches* (Revelation 2:17). For too long the church has not heard from God. She has relied upon someone to hear for her.

Jesus desires for us to step into unhindered, deep, passionate fellowship with Him. He wants us so reliant upon Him, knowing his amazing love. His voice, his plans, and his work must lead us within this world. We as the bride must be the perfect representation of his glory.

James 2:23 (esv) used to burn in me when I saw the words, 'He [Abraham] was called a friend of God.' My heart's cry was, "Lord, I want to be your friend." So often, I thought about my relationship with a good friend. I knew her likes and dislikes. I knew the things on her heart for that day. I asked Jesus, "Lord, I know what is in your Word, but what is on your heart today? What do you want to say today?"

People continually told me that what God wants to say today is in the Word. Definitely, I agree, everything that God wants to say is contained in his Word. He will never move from that or outside that, but I still was not satisfied. I wanted fresh manna from Heaven. I wanted to know what Jesus Christ wanted to say personally to Lana today. I was so tired of hearing big-name leaders in the Christian world say things like, "Jesus told me," or "Jesus placed such and such on my heart."

Through my journey, I learnt that it is all about making ourselves available. We position ourselves to hear from Jesus. It will cost us greatly, but it is so worth it. We will then be transformed by his radical love, beautiful Spirit, and magnificent voice.

I have learnt keys that have helped me grow in my journey of learning to hear from Jesus, and I want to share these with you. This is not a six-step plan on how to hear God's voice. These are simply pointers or keys that I pray will help you in your walk with Jesus as you grow in knowing Him and hearing his voice.

Above all, I believe that Jesus is calling his church to echo the prayer of Samuel in 1 Samuel 3:9 always:

"Speak, Lord, for your servant is listening."

L—Learn to maintain your time with the Lord. Choose a time every day to spend with Jesus. Maintain your relationship with the Lord. Consistently meet with Him, desiring to hear his voice. Do it daily, and the Lord will teach you to hear his voice. Make yourself available to Jesus to hear his voice. The Lord will not turn away a hungry heart that is seeking to hear his voice. Oh, how he will shower you in his love. Without these times daily, your relationship with the Lord can become stagnant and dry, and you will not know his voice for yourself. The Lord speaks to people who make themselves available to Him (Mark 1:35).

I—Indulge in the Word. Allow his Word to speak to you. Ask the Spirit to speak to you through his Word. This is the most common way that God speaks (Psalm 119).

S—Silence (Zephaniah *1:7*). Spend time soaking in his presence. You can do this through worship. Quiet your heart before the Lord. Lay down all your worries and expectations, and ask the Lord to speak to your heart. In a world that is full of distraction, we are constantly on the go unless we take the time to remain silent before the Lord. We will be influenced by many voices and not hear his still small voice within us. If silence is not a regular part of your relationship with the Lord, just soaking, start small—five or ten minutes a day—and build up as you are able. Do not feel condemned or guilty if your mind wanders, but just catch your mind, bring it back, and focus on Him. He loves you, and he will honor your heart's desire to just be with Him.

T—Thank the Lord for his promises of Him enabling us to hear his voice. Never lose your thankful heart (Psalm 138:1–3).

E—Expect Him to speak. Expect the Lord to be faithful to that which he has spoken (Psalm 38:15), and educate yourself on the ways that the Lord speaks (Job 33:14). The Lord can speak in various ways.

1. He will always speak through his Word. He will never contradict Himself.

2. He can speak in an audible voice as he did in 1 Samuel

3. He speaks in an internal voice into our hearts and into our minds.

4. The Lord speaks through the world. The beauty of creation testifies to God Himself (Romans 1:19–20).

5. He speaks through visions and dreams (Numbers 12:6, Acts 22:17–18).

6. The Lord may also appear before us as in Acts 9.

7. He can speak through impressions, or through a knowing (Nehemiah 7:5).

8. He also speaks through signs, nudges, books, children, newspaper headlines, movie names, circumstances, prophetic dramas, even through some people's lives.

N—Never stop meeting with Jesus. If the Lord does not speak in the way you desire, do not give up. The Lord will speak in the way he chooses and if you are continually quieting your heart, seeking to know Him and hear his voice he will speak   to you. The Lord desires to speak to you more than you want to hear Him. He may speak to you through *a* person he sends, but learn to listen to Him yourself and he will act. The great news since Jesus' death and resurrection is that we are all able to hear directly from God as his beloved children (Romans 8:14–16, 26–27).

It is so important to note that God will never ever contradict his Word (1 Corinthians 14:37). He is always consistent with his character (James 3:17). The fruit of God's voice is good (Matthew 7:15–23), and his voice is different from ours (Isaiah 55:8–9).

When I was learning to hear his voice, I simply sat before Him and asked Him to speak to me. I heard Him speak to me in small words like, "I love you." For the first few months I was frustrated because I thought; *I know God loves me, so God must be saying something more profound to me than that.* Yet every time I asked Him to speak, all I heard was, "I love you." I asked Him to reveal more of Himself to me through the Word.

It finally dawned on me: that maybe this *was* God speaking to me. Little did I realize that in those three little words was the most profound revelation. The love of God is something that cannot be grasped completely by our human minds and hearts while we are on this earth. I tested these little words that popped into my heart by lining them up with the Word. They did not contradict his Word or his character, so I took them into my heart.

Now, for you, the Lord may not speak to you in words or pictures all the time. He may choose to speak to you through reading his Word. He may give you a strong insight into a situation (also known as the gift of wisdom or gift of knowledge) as I have mentioned previously. What Jesus is looking for is the expectant hearts of his bride to hear Him speak.

I have always thought communication with Jesus is similar to the dialogue that I have with my husband, Kevin. If I went days upon days without speaking to Kevin, things would get pretty tense. There would obviously be a lot of miscommunication, and I would miss out on hearing Kevin's heart. I would not be a part of what is happening in his heart.

It is the same with our relationship with Jesus. Jesus has a lot more grace for us than we have for our spouses or any human relationship. The beautiful treasure we have in being able to hear Jesus speak to us is that we are then drawn **into** his heart. We can hear all that is on his heart and what is happening within his heart. What a privilege. Think about that for a moment. Jesus Christ the Son of God welcomes us into his heart to hear his secrets and share what is on his heart. Is there any greater privilege?

It is all about our hunger to hear his voice. Jesus will not turn a deaf ear to a hungry heart willing to sacrifice whatever it takes to hear his voice. That is where we are given another key to unlocking deeper communication with Jesus in our lives — sacrifice!

When I began my walk with Jesus, I read my Bible because that was my duty as a Christian. That was expected, and I wanted to know more about Jesus, of course. However, I was lacking the hunger and desperation to hear Jesus speak to me personally. I did it more out of wanting to be accepted by God and because I was told I had to, rather than out of that desperate hunger and to know his love.

Finally, as I started my journey seeking to hear his voice, I was willing to give anything to hear Him speak. I was so frustrated simply relying on the pastor to hear God for me and deliver it to me in a Sunday service. Then I had to wait a whole six days to hear God again. It propelled me into a greater hunger to hear his voice.

That is where sacrifice came in. Through a simple prayer of frustration, "Lord, I *know* there is more than this; I *know* that you want to speak to me daily. I open myself up to hear from you. Show me how to hear from you. Teach me how to tune my ears to your Spirit. Make me hungry for your presence. Make me want to hear your voice, Lord." In that instant, even though I did not realize straight away, the hunger began increasing.

The frustration I was feeling was the beginning of the hunger within me. That simple heart cry propelled me forward into the most glorious journey of my life—discovering his voice to me. It can be the same for you if you simply open your heart and invite the Spirit in at a deeper level to fine tune your ears to his Spirit.

My prayer of frustration was an actual declaration of my desire to hear only the Lord. One must be careful not to wait upon the Lord without protection, which would open the spirit to any voice that comes whispering. For example: I pray and make sure that I am wearing the armor of God. I bind any plan of the enemy to hinder me or interrupt me, and I cover myself with the blood of Jesus. When I do those things, I know that the enemy cannot come to whisper negative things in my ears.

I hear God as a thought in my mind that I did not put there, or a scripture in full quotation, scripture reference, or a picture. When God speaks it will always come with peace, you may not always get a "full sentence" from Him; you may just hear a word. Just remember there is no rush in a few minutes to understand what God is saying. Sometimes God may drop a word into my heart that won't leave me, and I will go weeks without knowing what it means. However, I will pray about it and eventually God shows me the meaning. Just be open to hear his voice and pray about what you hear, especially when you do not understand.

Make sure you always pray that the Lord would give you discerning of spirits to know his voice and to silence any voices that are not of Him. Remember he will never contradict his Word. Always pray for God to confirm his words to you.

Test the words that you hear. If you think you are hearing something radical or directional from Jesus like,

"Go sell your house," or "Move to Africa," here are a few suggestions in weighing those words.

These steps can also be used for anything that you hear from the Lord that you are not sure about.

1. Write it down.

2. Check it alongside the Word of God. If it contradicts the Word, throw it out immediately.

3. Take the word to your leaders or trusted friends who walk in wisdom and are in tune with the Spirit and talk to them.

4. Ask God to show you people you can share with in your life. Usually your word will witness with their spirit if they are in tune with the Holy Spirit.

5. The Holy Spirit will not speak one thing to you and another to your advisor if he is listening to Him.

6. Do not rush into anything and make any hasty decisions. Ask the Lord to bring clear confirmations to you.

7. After all these steps always let peace be your guide. The Holy Spirit will always bring peace and godly conviction, which is the leading of the Spirit to obey his Word, with words he gives you.

Anything that you hear from God should fit into one of three categories:

1.Encouragement—a word God speaks to you or to someone else through you will always encourage. It will always spur them to grow closer to Jesus.

2.Edification—the word will always build your relationship with Jesus and make you stronger in Him. It will take you from glory to glory.

3.Exhortation—the word will push you forward in seeking deeper relationship with Jesus.

Even if the Lord convicts you of sin, he will never condemn. He will always speak with love in a way that will carry you to a greater level of freedom and peace. He will encourage you to seek Him deeply and to walk in holiness.

Do not be afraid to be wrong. It is better to hear and step out than to not hear and never move. Start with baby steps. If you hear the Lord telling you to call a friend and encourage that person with a verse, step out and do it. If you are wrong, who cares? At least you tried!

Many times, I have heard wrong or I have misinterpreted what Jesus has said to me, and you know what? That is okay! You learn by trying. Our fleshly desires can speak to us and so can the enemy, but be encouraged. Always ask the Lord for clarification and interpretation by asking the Holy Spirit to confirm what he has shown you in his Word and give you clear direction about what to do with what you hear.

If it does not come straight away, keep asking and do not move forward until you have some sort of direction from God on its meaning and interpretation. You may receive the direction from the Word of God, or through a godly friend or mentor. If you are really struggling about what to do with what you hear, take it to your pastor or someone further along in maturity. God will lead you when you have an open heart to obey Him. He will not leave you wondering forever. He will speak to you.

Let me give you an example. I prayed to hear from Jesus about ministry opportunities. I dreamt that a pastor I know called me. I saw him on the phone to me, and then I woke up. I suddenly thought he was calling me to ask me to preach. I got so excited and kept waiting for the phone to ring. It did not ring.

Then I saw him at his church, and guess what, he still did not ask me. Instead, he told me how the numbers in his night service had dwindled. I was so upset. I went to the Lord and said, "But, Lord, you said that he was going to call me and ask me to preach!"

I heard Jesus speak to me, "No, I did not say that. This dream was to alert you that he needed your prayer support and your encouragement."

I had misinterpreted what Jesus was trying to tell me in the dream. I only discovered what Jesus was trying to convey to me when I actually asked Him. We must always seek clarification and confirmation from Jesus. As you can see there was no harm done in this situation. It was just a lesson from the Lord about how we are always to check with Him. The interpretation we think we have might not always be what the Lord is trying to say.

Jesus may allow circumstances in our lives to fine tune our hearing. When they come, we rejoice in them because although they are frustrating and hurt for a moment, they bring great joy in the long run. Hearing from Jesus takes time, and it takes effort, patience, and sacrifice. At times it takes waiting. Do not give up a hungry heart to hear more from Jesus. Do not give up seeking and asking the Lord to speak. If you continue to do those things you are on the path to knowing how to hear Him more.

The hungrier we are to hear his voice, the more we are willing to sacrifice. You have heard the words, or maybe you have said it, "I will do anything to get that." That is what Jesus is looking for in the hearts of his people right now. He is looking for desperate people who are willing to sacrifice whatever they need to in order to hear his voice. Your sacrifice might be time, or it might be a job. It might be a television show, friendships, unrepented sin, or unforgiveness. There are many things that can hinder us from hearing the Lord. Is there something in your life that is hindering you from hearing the Lord's voice?

For me, it was time. I was so busy all the time, I did not have one minute to sit before the Lord and listen. I was always on the run, and then I crashed and burned into a heap of frustration, wondering why God was not speaking to me. All the time the ball was in my court. I just had to position myself.

I sacrificed time with friends, time reading, and I sat before Jesus with an open Bible. I told Him I was not going to move until I heard Him speak. Believe me, my mind wandered many times. Do not feel condemned if your mind wanders. It happens to all of us. It is just a matter of continually bringing your mind back onto Jesus and focusing on Him and his Word.

Day after day I sat before the Lord and asked Him to speak. At first it was twenty minutes or thirty minutes to simply hear the words, "I love you." Sometimes I came across a verse that touched me deeply. Oftentimes that verse had never been touched me before. The more I sacrificed what I called luxuries in my life to learn to hear Jesus speak, the more he honored my heart's cry.

Do not ever let anyone tell you that Jesus will not speak to you. That is the greatest lie around. Jesus wants to communicate with you more than you want to hear. Do not become frustrated if you do not hear Him straight away. It takes time, but you position yourself before Him and he *will* meet you. He is faithful (1 Corinthians 1:9).

Jesus is calling his bride to live like Martha's sister, Mary in Luke 10:39–42. She knew the priority and importance of sitting before Jesus and hearing his heart. Jesus said that she chose the most important thing. I don't know about you, but I have always wondered what Jesus was saying to her. Was he telling her how important it was to maintain fellowship with Him as she was doing and not to be consumed by making things right for Him? We just have to read Luke 10 and see that it is all about our being before Him.

God is not looking for people who are going to do things for Him. He is looking for people who are desperate to hear his heart, grow in knowing his love, and follow his lead to do that which he calls them to do. If we cannot hear what the Spirit is saying, how do we know where the Spirit is leading? We are given guidance in the Word of God, but the Lord also wants us living moment by moment hearing what the Spirit is saying. If we are not listening for what the Spirit is saying, then we guess what he wants us to do. We move forward on our own assumptions. It is crucial that we, the body of Christ, learn how to nestle ourselves under his wing and listen to what his heart is saying.

Jesus wants to speak to you! He loves you immensely so he always wants to draw you closer to Him. That is the plain and unshakeable truth. Jesus wants to teach you how to hear his voice, which will propel you into deeper levels of relationship with Him.

I have mentioned earlier, it all started with a frustration and hunger for hearing God's voice. I did not want to stay where I was. I wanted more. I wanted to be in constant communication with Jesus. There was not any evidence in the Word against that. I pursued it with all my strength and I did not give up until Jesus spoke to me.

Some days I did not hear Him at all. I sat before Him desperate to hear what the Spirit was saying, yet I heard nothing. Here is where the rubber hits the road. This is a point of decision. We can decide to claim that the Lord does want to speak to his children, or we can decide to prevent the enemy from coming in with accusing thoughts.

It is all about the small steps. It is all about not giving up. It is all about continually praying for Jesus to increase the hunger within you. We need to keep seeking and sacrificing. Jesus is not hiding up in heaven. He is not watcting his children seek Him desperately while he plans not to reveal Himself. When we desperately come to Him, he comes to us and embraces us with open arms.

Let us continue to examine our hearts and our lives to see if there is anything in our lives that could clog our ears. One of the greatest clogs in today's church is complacency. Complacency says, "I am comfortable where I am, and I choose to remain in this place. I am not desperate enough to sacrifice my comfort in order to grow." Blunt? Yes, but true. If we find ourselves in a place of complacency, it is because we are comfortable where we are and not very hungry. Seeing more of who Jesus Christ is, hearing his voice, and seeing his heart shatters all complacency because we cannot live in dynamic relationship with Jesus Christ without being changed.

Jesus does not want just a one-way conversation; Jesus wants us to hear his heart too.

"Very early the next morning, Jesus got up and went to a place where he could be alone and pray." Mark 1:35 (cev)

Here I believe is a model of relationship, Jesus was demonstrating the relationship. We are called to maintain and prioritize our relationship with Jesus above all. Jesus may challenge you to get up at the crack of dawn. He did to me for a season. I got up at five in the morning to seek Him. It was so difficult at times, yet it was very rewarding. The challenge in this verse is really to prioritize your time spent with Jesus above all else.

You will prioritize your main focus in life. Jesus is to be our focus. He takes precedence, so our times with Him must follow suit.

Jesus is calling us to step up to **live** in the secret place— a place of constantly hearing Jesus' voice and following his lead. We are not to dip in and out of it. It is possible to remain with Him all the time because he lives within us, and talking with Him during the day, recognizing his presence, and just enjoying Him draws us closer to Him. I have not attained this place yet. However, the more I exercise the principles I have mentioned, the more I grow in hearing his voice, and flowing in his Spirit daily.

Jesus wants the Bride to learn to live like this. We may all hear Jesus in different ways, but the foundational truth is Jesus speaks to every one of us. We just need to learn how to listen and allow the Spirit to reveal to us the way that he is speaking.

"My sheep listen to my voice; and I know them, and they follow me." John 10:27 (esv)

Want to be a world changer? I know I do. This world

is not going to be changed by people who go to church on a Sunday and hear the Word of God from the pastor if that is the extent of their growing in God and hearing from Him. I am not discounting teaching from the pulpit, it is extremely important to our growth as Christians, but if this is the only input you are receiving from the Lord into your life, then I want to encourage you to really pursue his voice for yourself as well. This world is going to be changed by those of us who are answering the call, the mandate being placed before us by the Spirit of God. It will be changed by those of us who are desperately hungering for more of Jesus. Change will also come from our obedience to Him, our faithfulness and our continued service. This world will be changed by those of us who want to hear his voice and go after it with a whole heart. It is to be our number one priority.

Jesus is to be our number one priority. To put Him in the highest place in our lives means to give everything we have to know Him and learn to hear Him. It is a lifetime journey, but it is an exciting, adventurous, fulfilling journey. It will cost us everything, but what is everything compared to the glorious privilege of hearing the voice of Jesus Christ on an everyday basis? It doesn't compare! Hallelujah!

Prayer:
Father, in the name of Jesus, I thank you that you long to speak to me more than I want to hear from you. I thank you for your amazing love for me and the

privilege it is to hear your voice. Teach me to hear your voice more than I ever have before. Teach me how to listen. Help me to set aside time every day to seek you and to know you.

Show me a greater revelation of how to live in the secret place. I give everything to you, Lord. I open my heart to you now and ask you to increase the hunger in me to know you and hear your voice. I want to live my life by what I hear you saying. I love you, Lord.

I thank you that you have heard my prayer. In Jesus' name, amen.

Epilogue - The Dance That Lasts Forever

I felt led to include this last chapter. It is something that the Lord showed me on March 14, 2008. This is a final encouragement of what is burning on the heart of God. I have done my best to convey throughout this book a longing for intimacy with Jesus Christ. Dance with Him in your personal relationship now and through all eternity. That is his heart for you. Dive into knowing Him and his heart for you and his great love for you and oh how you shall be changed!

Friend, I have said it before, and I will say it again, "Let us have our focus purely on knowing who Jesus Christ is. Let us learn to know his heart, love, and his character. Let us learn to hear his voice and walk aligned with the Spirit

Lana Vawser

daily."

It is as we, his bride, step up to the call of intimacy with Him daily, that we will see an overflow from our lives that we have never seen before. It is not something that we can conjure, but as we swim in the ocean of intimacy with Jesus, we will see the Holy Spirit pour out his presence from our lives like we can only ever dream. As he said, there will be rivers of living waters flowing from our innermost beings (John 7:37).

I enjoy walking this journey with you. Together we grow in our hunger, desperation and passion to know Jesus Christ intimately and hear his voice. Let this journey not stop here. Let the encouragement and voice of God that flows through these pages burn on our hearts for all of eternity.

May we see this world changed as his Bride becomes a people who truly know Him and his heart. May we walk in his ways, void of complacency, and truly seeking Him above all else.

Always seeking Him,

—Lana Vawser

Invitation Word

My precious church, I am calling you to a depth of intimacy that you have not known before. I am calling you to come to me and truly shake off all things that hinder you from greater intimacy with me. I love you; I greatly love you. Come and know my love. Let me show you my heart of love for you.

Many of you sing songs of praise and walk

in a greater depth of worship than you have ever known before. Many of you hear the heartbeat of my heart. You hear the song that I am releasing and answer the call of deeper intimacy with me. I am well pleased.

Many of you also sing songs of ministry and sing songs of future events. I speak to you today, my church. Take your focus off of these things and place them on me. When your eyes are on things other than me, you can miss what I am trying to speak unto you.

I have released a fire upon my church. It is a fire of desperate hunger to draw you closer to me. Many of you allow the fire to go out through distraction, busyness, anxiety, and worry. Do not let the fire go out; press into me. Seek me as you have never sought me before, and I will answer you.

I am not far from you, I am here, my church, and I desire to take you to a place of intimacy you have not known before. It is in the stillness of my presence that you are changed and transformed into my image. Many of you await breakthrough, guidance, and wisdom, but I speak unto you, my church, that you will not receive these things if you are not pressing closer to me.

For what is more important? To receive from me what you desire or to know my heart? I raise up those who are willing to hear and know what it means to entertain my presence. Those who know what it means to feast upon my Word deeply and not just nibble.

In the coming days many of you will receive greater impartation of my Spirit through your time with me. I am not calling you to be legalistic in your times with me. No, I am calling you to hear the Spirit. I am calling you higher. Step up by allowing my Spirit to create this great hunger and desperation within your hearts.

You are not to be smoldering wicks, my church, but blazing bushels of my glory. Lay aside your distractions. Lay aside your worries and come to dance and rejoice with your beloved. Come to rejoice in the one whom your heart truly desires. It is through repentance from swayed intentions, focus, and vision that I will draw you closer to me. You will see me as you have never seen me before.

The time has come when the move of my Spirit is increasing in the hearts of those who are truly hearing. I did not call you to be a deaf church. I called you to be a church that lives in my heart and listens to my heartbeat.

Sweet bride, hear my voice. Hear me as I call you higher. Hear me calling you to lay aside all distractions and embrace the invitation to come up high. Lay aside worldly plans and empty promises and allow your heart to receive the tune of my heart.

Listen to what my heart is singing. It is singing for you, my bride.

Come deeper. Come higher. Come closer. Come nearer.

I love you. Come and let me show you more of my love for you.

Hear my heart. Feast on my Word, and allow my Spirit to teach you in greater degrees how to hear my voice. The sweet honey of my presence is being released upon those who are hungry, those who are willing, and those who have heard.

Let not your fire be snuffed out, my bride. Walk in repentance, shake off all that hinders, and come forward to see the beauty of who I am. See more deeply the love I have for you. Embrace more passionately the revelation of who I am. Come to sit before me. Wave not your times with me before man, but meet with me in the quiet, and you will forever be changed.